GROWING
IN A
WELSH VALLEY

Kathleen Healy

ARTHUR H. STOCKWELL LTD.
Elms Court   Ilfracombe   Devon
Established 1898

© *Kathleen Healy, 1999*
First published in Great Britain, 1999
All rights reserved.
No part of this publication may be reproduced or transmitted in any form or by any means, electronic or mechanical, including photocopy, recording, or any information storage and retrieval system, without permission in writing from the copyright holder.

British Library Cataloguing-in-Publication Data.
A catalogue record for this book is available from the British Library.

Illustrations set between pages 32-33
Other illustrations pages 4 and 60

ISBN 0 7223 3206-8
Printed in Great Britain by
Arthur H. Stockwell Ltd.
Elms Court   Ilfracombe
Devon

CONTENTS

Chapter 1	7
Chapter 2 — "The Graig"	13
Chapter 3	17
Chapter 4	34
Chapter 5	47
Chapter 6	52
Poems: 'My Childhood Home'	58
'Mother'	59
'The Boy I knew at School'	59

The author at seventeen

Author's Preface

I am now seventy-six years of age and have attempted to write about my 'Childhood Memories' which cover the period from 1925 to 1940 when I lived in Pontardawe.

As all my recollections are from memory, no doubt some will be slightly amiss, in which case, I can only apologise and hope that my sequence of events in the small mining town of Pontardawe will be of interest to those mentioned therein, their relatives and students alike.

Kathleen Healy

Chapter One

My earlier recollections would have been around the age of three years, in 1925. I was born in my granfer's house in Ynisderw Road on the 28th May 1922 and we moved to a new Council house, number 36 in the village of Trebanos when I was two years of age. Our house was the last house at the cul-de-sac end of a long row of neat houses in this small village in the Swansea Valley.

We had farm fields to the side of us, and our road lay behind the main road, which took you to Swansea, about six miles in one direction and up the valley to Brecon and further in the opposite direction.

The houses lining the sides of the main road were mainly detached, very nicely kept, with pretty front gardens. These houses, cushioned us from the noise of the traffic, so it was fairly quiet, and we could play safely, either in the farmer's fields or on the pavement outside our house. My sister Mary, who was eighteen months older than I was, my mother and my father, made up our family at that time, and a very happy family we were.

My mother came to Pontardawe as a "baby in arms" with her mother, father and widowed grandmother on her mother's side. They were originally from Llandilo-Tal-y-Bont-Pontardulais. Granfer Richards, Mam's father, was a builder and stonemason by trade and lived in one of the houses, in the row of houses he had built in Ynisderw Road — leading towards the steelworks. I don't know where the family lived before he built the row of houses. He named these houses "May Cottages 1892", after my mother and her year of birth.

He was a tall, quiet, composed man, with a kind smile. He employed three or four men, and besides houses, he built the Grammar School and the Technical College in Pontardawe and another school on the corner of the main road in Alltwen, named Alltwen Primary School.

They were to know great sadness, when Mam was twelve years old;

the eldest child of six children; her mother died in childbirth, with the sixth child surviving. Mam had one sister, Elizabeth, and four brothers — Wilfred, Edgar, William Arthur and Daniel, he being christened the day of his mother's funeral. Mam's grandmother was a widow, named Margaret Williams whose husband had been a shoemaker (Williams y Crudd) and she lived with the family and now had her hands full with only Mam to help to bring up the young family.

My father, was a native of "Abbey Side", Dungarvan, County Waterford in Southern Ireland. He was fifteen years of age, when he came over to live with his aunt and uncle in Ynisderw Road, and to look for work. His elder brother, Michael, preceded him a few years earlier, for the same reason, looking for work. They lived a few doors away from Mam with Mr and Mrs McGrath, their mother's brother Michael McGrath.

Dad found work with the GPO as a telegram boy. His aunt and uncle had a young daughter, named Helen; she was six years of age, and she was the "apple of their eyes!" Suddenly she had two big cousins from Ireland to tease her. She adored them all her life until suddenly this was to change.

When the war broke out in 1914, cousin Michael was one of the first "Pontardawe" boys who volunteered to join the Army to fight for "King and Country". He became a sergeant with the "2nd Battalion Royal Munster Fusiliers", and died of wounds on the 2nd March 1917, aged twenty-five years, after winning the MM and BAR, the DCM and the Albert Medal; the family believed he was the only Irishman to win the Albert Medal.

Grandma Healy came over from Ireland to Buckingham Palace, where King George V presented her with Michael's "Albert Medal", and the following is the verbatim extract from the *London Gazette* dated 4th July 1917.

July 4th 1917

The "Gazette" of July 4th just published, contains the following official version of the deed which brought Sergeant Michael Healy, of the Munster Fusiliers, the Albert Medal, and which also cost him his life:

Sergeant Michael Healy, Munster Fur.

In France, during bombing practice a live bomb rolled back into the trench, which was occupied by the thrower, an officer, and Sergeant Healy. All three ran for shelter, but Sergeant Healy, fearing the others would not reach shelter in time, ran back and picked up the bomb, which exploded and mortally wounded him. Healy had previously performed other acts of distinguished gallantry, for which he had been awarded the DCM, the MM and a BAR to the MM.

The Distinguished Conduct Medal was presented to Sergeant Healy for capturing a machine gun and five Germans single-handed.

The Albert Medal, which cost him his life, was presented to Sergeant Healy's mother, Mrs James Healy of County Waterford, Ireland, at Buckingham Palace by King George V.

The king in his conversation with Mrs Healy, remarked he was extremely sorry he did not have the honour of shaking hands with Sergeant Healy himself. "Be proud of him," he said "he was a brave boy."

Sergeant Healy was a Pontardawe boy, and as will be seen by the above report, has won no less than four military distinctions.

We understand Uncle Michael did not die until the following day at the Field Hospital; he was unable to speak, but his eyes searched all who came near him. It was the second day when a Catholic priest came in. He smiled at the priest who gave him the last rites, and he passed away immediately. His name is recorded on the Pontardawe War Memorial, near the Public Hall, Herbert Street, and his decorations are listed after his name.

My father also served in the Great War, but, he never wanted to enlarge on that period — maybe had we been sons he would have "opened-up" the conversation.

Mam and Dad were married when he joined the Army and I remember seeing a picture of them (sepia), with Dad in uniform, holding his peaked cap with a brass regimental badge in the front, slightly under his arm, head held high as if to attention. Mam wore a long-sleeved V-neck blouse, a nice woollen A-line skirt and fashionable double bar shoes.

At this time, they were living in rooms at "Granfer's". They did so for the first two years, then moved to their first house in Trebanos, and having worked for a while as a builder's labourer for Granfer Richards, he got a job in the Pontardawe steelworks at the furthest end of Ynisderw Road. His responsibility was to shovel coal for the boilers, which in turn, kept up the pressure in the powerhouse, to the necessary level and very hard manual work it was. The palms of his hands were hard and scarred, and after his daily bath, with regularity, he would gently rub a "thick yellow grease" into these cracks and into his fingers. He was always a happy man, making us laugh, and often tried to "catch us out" with one of his "riddle-me-rees", seeing if we were able to guess who or what he was supposed to be?

He had a large accordion, which he played from memory; he was never taught. Everyone played the accordion where he came from; you just "picked it up" as one of the family "put it down", and had a go! His Irish reels went faster and faster. There was always music in our house. Other days he would play his serious music, beautiful ballads. Myself, I learned most of the words, and would still be humming the tune long after the accordion was put away. My mother hummed her favourite music pieces too, mainly hymns, and they too, gave me a warm feeling inside of me, a feeling of calm and happiness.

We had been living in this Council house for about two years, when early one morning, about 6 a.m. on the 27th August 1927, my father woke me up and holding my hand in his, and my sister Mary's with the other, he took us into the back bedroom, where my mother was propped up on her pillows, and wrapped snugly by her side was a baby, all "pink and fair". I now had a baby sister — she was like my doll, but nicer; although she cried quite a lot!

As we left my mother's side, my father took us into the empty "boxroom", which was never used; it was too small; and there in a corner — was a 'hen' with a brood of little yellow chicks! So that to me, was a lovely day indeed. Two surprises in one day!

The New Arrival

Come with me my father said one morning, just 'fore dawn.
He took me to my mother's side to see the baby, newly born.
My mother looked at me and smiled, her smile was just for me —
You see we shared a secret of her promise made to me.
'Twas weeks before, when I lay in bed and she sang me off to sleep,
She promised me a baby, my very own, to keep.
And here it was, all pink and fair, wrapped snugly by her side.
'Twas like my doll, but nicer, though my doll she never cried.
At first, I liked my sister, though she did cry a lot
And she got all the hugs and kisses, like the ones I always got!
I did not get as many; no, I don't think I did;
I did not like her for a while, till my father said I should.
I stayed close to Mother and I watched her all the time;
I watched her feed my sister, this baby who was mine.
And then I grew to love her, though I suppose I always did,
And I was five and older and now so very big.
I helped my mam to wash her, and she splashed me from her bath;
I knew then it was nice to have her, and I settled down at last.

The new baby was named Annie Enid. She was born the month before I started school, and Annie was the name of our Irish grandmother.

Starting school, was a big day for me. I was nervous before I left the house, but my sister Mary was almost two years older than me, and told me we were to keep to the pavement all the way, because it was a busy main road. Even so, I was on the outside and I had to stop several times to pull up my socks; and eventually we reached the school entrance gates. In front of me, must have been thirty wide steps leading up to the school, where Mary deposited me at the infants' block, behind the main school, but still within the grounds, and left me. Fear gripped me again. I thought I was the new child, but we were all new children starting school.

We were soon seated and our names checked. Then we were occupied in various activities. We sat at our small desks for a while with our slates and chalk, drawing and copying what our teacher had put on her blackboard. Then a bell rang, and we all filed into the playground — where I found my sister, and once she saw I was all right, she returned to her own playground below, and play break was over for the morning.

My school days were enjoyable. Children I played with outside our house, were also in my class, and some evenings after meal time, we were able to get together again and play games for a short while.

Other times, we would be taught our "Arithmetic Tables" in the house, where we had a large blackboard and chalk, and our parents made it all seem exciting. We were able to recite our Arithmetic Tables almost as poems, although at times Mam would suddenly ask how much is ? x ? and I would have to mentally run through that number until I arrived at the answer, then write it on the blackboard. Lessons were fun, and I adored Arithmetic.

The Christmas which followed my starting school, was to be one I could never forget. We put our stockings up where Father Christmas would see them, and in the morning, not only did he leave us our orange, nuts, sweets and our beloved "golliwog", but laying in a large box was the most beautiful china headed doll I had ever seen; almost the size of a baby. My doll was dressed in blue and Mary's in pink. The dolls had pretty curls, long eyelashes, pretty teeth and you could even see her tiny tongue.

After breakfast, our friends Nellie Bolton and her sister Evelyn, came out with their presents and I asked whether I could take my doll outside, and bring it back indoors straight away? I was holding her very carefully, when one of the children, a boy from the main road, who sometimes came through the farm field to join us, grabbed my doll, hit her head on the concrete gate post — then gave her back to me. I howled and I was scolded, and both Mam and Dad told me I would never have another doll ever again; and I never did. No amount of explaining how it happened would calm my parents. It upset them both, and I never saw the broken doll again.

Mary's doll lasted much longer, it was passed down to my sister Enid and for some years it was treasured until accidentally it fell off the bed when Enid was ill with measles, and tossing and turning; it came to a sorry end. Dad had saved precious shillings all the year so that Mary and I could have these beautiful china headed dolls.

The New Year saw "The Depression" and Dad was out of a job. He could not find work. Food was costly when your parents only have the "dole" allowance. My mother became ill, because the baby was not thriving. The doctor seemed to be forever "listening" to the child's breathing, chest and back, and in the end told my parents, they may not be able to raise the child as she was a sickly baby.

Nearby, in the next village of Clydach, was the Mond Nickel works. Not a flower grew anywhere around this area, due to the fumes which left the chimney stacks continually. The doctor thought this might be the reason for my mother's ill health too, and he suggested we try and find a house on a hillside away from the works. At that time, there were many complaints regarding people's health due to these fumes.

Chapter Two — "The Graig"

And so, we moved, still in Trebanos, but about three miles further up the valley. On a hillside, there were a pair of band-new houses; detached, gardens back and front, and we moved into one of these. The area was known as "The Graig", Trebanos, and it took the same time to get to school, although a little longer returning, as it was all "uphill".

So now, we were to breathe cleaner air? Poor Mam! Little did she know then, that the constant complaints regarding the fumes from the Mond Nickel works, damaging the people's health, the firm were instructed to heighten the chimney stacks to take the fumes away from the village, but, at the same time, they carried the fumes to the hillside — so the air was not cleaner, as Mam thought.

She was yet to experience many more obstacles. Dad's income (the dole) after he being ill for a while, was exactly £1.9s.0d (£1.45) and every Monday morning, the owner called for his rent money — nine shillings, (45p). The dole was £1.6s.0d (£1.30) for husband and wife and one shilling (5p) for each child x three made it the princely sum of £1.9s.0d.

The newly built house was a three-bedroom, bathroom, kitchen, living room, with an enormous range for cooking and a small parlour on the opposite side of the stairs. There was a separate brick building outside, quite spacious, housing a flush toilet. The rear garden was higher than the house, and a flight of steps to the left gave access to quite a large plot of land, where we were to keep poultry and grow vegetables. At the opposite side, and at the front of the house, was a sloping grassy bank, leading down to the gate. A similar house stood next to ours, giving ample room between the two houses; yet we were huddled to the hillside. The living room range was in use every day as it was the source of plenty of boiling water. A couple of large saucepans and a large black kettle, took pride of place on top of the highly black-leaded grate and hob. It also had a boiler with a brass tap, and a large oven for baking.

Below our house, were other homes, and a rough country road down to the village and our school. Lanes ran in different directions ending at farms or cottages. One lane nearby, took you to Tyn-y-Pant Farm. This lane was shaded by tall trees, to the side of which ran a shallow stream and a grassy bank above it. This was where I loved to stray and look at masses of bluebells beside the tallest stemmed violets I had ever seen. I loved "The Graig".

Everything was perfect, completely different to the Council estate. Here, we saw "wildlife" and came to recognise the various birds which seemed to be around all day. I watched them in the holidays, fetching wisps of grass and moss for their nests, and was delighted to find Jenny Wren, one of the smallest of wild birds, build her nest in the bank of the hillside and cap it with a lid, lift the lid and settle inside. My parents had stressed I should not touch any nests I came across, as the mother bird would discard it and any eggs would be ruined. Many times I saw a fox. He would be looking for food. Some nights the chicken house would be raided and the spoils would be seen scattered about, feathers everywhere. Hedgehogs loved the countryside too and we loved the way they protected themselves if they happened to be anywhere near our dog, when he was free of his kennel! Try as he might, he could never get them to unfurl from the tight ball they had rolled themselves into, but evidence showed the dog, had tried to sniff them, as his head was always showing fleas from the contact with them; that meant the "flea" powder was kept near at hand, always!

Gypsies called from time to time, selling pegs or heather, and there was always a baby wrapped up in a shawl on their back. I believe they sensed my mother was nervous of them, they were not in any hurry to move on. We were, of course, the last of two houses nestling against the cliff edge of the Graig; although opposite us, but on the lower ground, were a family with about seven boys; one David, worked at the farm above us. The family were of Pentecostal faith.

The gypsies, knew Mam would make them some tea, or give them some of her lemonade which they waited for, as they rested on the grassy bank at the side of our house. "Keep your eyes on them" she used to say to me, "they will steal anything they can lay their hands on!" Hedgehogs made a fulfilling meal they told us — completely covered in clay — they roasted them in the hot ashes of a fire, and they called them "roast whichy whichy". I used to feel so sorry for the poor hedgehogs. How did they multiply if the gypsies ate them, and others got squashed by traffic?

Mam never bought anything from them; she had no spare cash — but as soon as Dad would get indoors, she would tell him, "By the way, I'm running short of pegs!"

"Oh, the Romanies have been I guess?" and sure enough he would sit on the garden steps and whittle away at the wood, and make her some gypsy pegs!

My dad found a disused coal seam to the side of our neighbour's new house, and with this coal dust and clay, a large shovel and a bucket of water, he would mix enough to form a fairly firm compound, and form them into balls and leave them to dry at the back of the house. Once the range was started, these additional balls kept the fire going; and it cost nothing. It was known as "Pele".

Dad was still hoping to get work, and being strong and healthy, he was prepared to go up to the farm on top of the Graig to work, if there was any, whilst "The Depression" lasted. He was not allowed to accept payment, but payment in kind — "foodstuff". He was given work at Pen-y-Graig Farm and some evenings we saw him bring home dairy produce, vegetables in plenty and sometimes a piece of "side of bacon". They gave him work whenever they needed help on the land. They knew him to be honest and reliable, and they always addressed him as Mr Healy.

It was whilst living on "The Graig", my father got a message from his family in Ireland. His mother was dying from cancer. Money was scarce, although he did get to see her before she died.

None of our family saw our Irish grandparents. We had photographs of them though. Whilst living at Granfer's, Grandma Healy came over to see us, and stayed with her brother and family, Michael McGrath. That was when I was a baby.

Three of my father's sisters, settled in Derbyshire and two married engine drivers on "The Express Trains", this enabling them to reap the benefit of "cheap fares" and to visit their parents regularly. Another sister, married a Scottish soldier, whose father was a laird, and as the eldest son, the title passed to him. He was Uncle Walter. He now moved into the house and grounds of "Alt Skay", in West Perthshire, and he became, for many years, the Royal Falconer. His picture was on sale at resorts and shops, dressed in the Scottish kilt and tammy, holding a falcon on his arm. He also sported a long beard.

It was soon after my Irish grandmother's death, that Dad's sister Sheila came over to stay with us for a couple of months. She was run down from nursing her mother. I believe she would have been possibly, twenty-one years of age. With her, came the most beautiful puppy, an Irish terrier. He was brown and white and she gave him to us girls as a present. We were delighted. He ran around constantly, and, of course, we chased him too, until he found a safe haven under the free-standing bath in the bathroom. We named him "Paddy". He was our first dog.

Mary and I were both given another present each, a "rosary". Mary's was amber in colour, mine was blue, and to this day, I never knew how my "lost rosary" was found in the chicken run at the top of the garden. It had been lost sometime, and I was never one to go near the henhouse. I hated the dry humidity which emanated around it. It suffocated me, so I kept well away.

I was sorry to see my aunt, Sheila, return home to Ireland. She was always telling us stories when we asked her to. Before she left for home, she told my dad that their father had had a premonition of brother Michael's death. Her father had gone into Dungarvan, in Waterford, one morning and had met up with some friends, and they stood on the bridge, talking. After a while, Granddad left and decided to take the "short cut" way home to their cottage, along the railway line. They were in charge of the gates on the railway crossing and had to "open" the gates for the express trains to go through, at certain times of the day. Ahead of him, he saw Michael in uniform with his rucksack on his shoulder. He called out to him "Michael, wait for me" — but Michael did not seem to hear him. He called louder and walked faster and still Michael did not stop, until he came to their cottage home, where he turned right and disappeared at the cottage.

Their father got home and said to their mother "Where is Michael? I've been behind him all the way and I called to him to wait for me, but he did not hear me."

"Well maybe he's gone down the garden to the lavvy."

But he was not there either, so both sat down and their mother said "Michael's dead. It is a forewarning", and a message was received soon after to say he had been killed.

Chapter Three

During the August school holidays and sometimes at other weekends, I delighted in visiting "Pen-y-Graig Farm", where Dad worked when it was a busy period. The three daughters, encouraged me to sleep there. I slept in a small room, which had been their grandmother's. It had a fair-sized bed, feathered mattress and feathered eiderdown! Margaretta, the second daughter of three, and Hannes the elder daughter, took me to bed in the evening, and each held my arm and leg, then dropped me onto the bed. I disappeared amongst the bedclothes, and we all laughed a lot. Hannes would sit me on her lap and hug me; of course, I wallowed in all this attention. I was about six years of age.

Margaretta spent quite some time in the dairy, making butter and cheese; and with two wooden platters, the butter was weighed, then stamped with a "cow" before being wrapped up for sale. The dairy was very large; a stone floor and rather chilly. The huge barrel which held the buttermilk was assessable any time I felt like a drink; it tasted slightly sour but one grew to like it. Hannes did all the housework and the meals. They had a brother, Hopkin, who worked on the land, and their younger sister, Ceinwen, preferred delivering the milk on the milk float. She was possibly around twenty years of age at this time. Their father was a little man, with "snow-white hair" and he was very pleasant, but never seemed to leave his armchair in the corner of the living room.

They had a large herd of milking cows; some milked by hand and others by machine. Collecting eggs was part of my chore, and some hens laid their eggs in most unusual places; many up in the hay loft!

One day, a lad helping out, put his hand into a sack of grain and got it caught in a rat trap! Pigs were the only animals I was scared of; they could be vicious and I was told to keep away from them as they would eat anything, and leave no trace behind! I disliked the smell of them too, so I did not need telling twice!

In the evening, when all the work had been done, the family would sit around a large fire and talk, and I sat with them and ate hot buttered toast and drank a glass of milk. The farm dog was a gold and white sheepdog. Her name was Tess; she was a pretty dog, gentle natured. Her coat always looked as though she had just been groomed. I'm sure she understood every word of the conversation and when asked to warm her feet, she was happy to perform, holding one paw towards the warmth of the fire, then the other one. Although it was summertime, there was always a fire, for cooking and hot water.

Ceinwen, the younger daughter, and Margaretta, took turns to prepare the milk float with huge churns of milk for the morning. The churns stood in the cooler in cold running water in the yard. Pint and half pint measures, hung to the churns, ready for delivery through to the next village of Trebanos where I lived in the Council house, a short time before. There were also crates of bottled milk. They were gradually changing over to bottling their milk.

I was very excited when they suggested I could now go along with one of them and a fifteen-year-old farmhand on the early-morning milk round. We were away by 6 a.m. and we went direct to the village of Trebanos without stopping. There the milk float was turned around not far from the cemetery, bordering the village of Clydach, and the placid old horse would stop at the different houses, which he knew from experience, while the milk was delivered. At the command of "walk on" the horse would walk the few yards to the next customer's house and stop. My place in the float, was "up front", holding onto the carved wooden headboard behind the horse as he trotted along until his round was finished and we made for home in Pontardawe. His pace would then be a little quicker, and it was a lovely experience, the wind in my face, just like riding in a chariot I imagined, only not as fast, and it never bothered me when he lifted his tail and left behind manure for some lucky person, who was quick with his bucket and spade. I could not have been happier than I was on these early-morning trips. This was the pattern of our daily deliveries whilst I holidayed at the farm.

One of the boys living opposite us, there were six of them, was named David. He was about sixteen years of age and helped on the farm and with the milk delivery round, and when I first started staying on the farm during my school holidays, he asked me one afternoon, if I would like a ride on the big broad carthorse, around the field. I was delighted and he led the horse by its collar after lifting me up on its broad back. Once out of sight, he started to force his hand inside the leg of my gym knickers, and I begged him to stop. He was hurting me, but he laughed, then kept pushing all his fingers inside my private parts. It was agony and I cried, but he kept smiling. It was the most painful thing I ever experienced and tears rolled down my face — but he continued doing it until we had gone around three sides of the square field. When we arrived back in the yard, Ceinwen, Margaretta and Hannes were standing there, they could see I was in a very distressed state and after telling him to lift me off the horse and to take the horse back to where he got it, and get on with his work, they took me into the house and asked me what he had done?

After I had told them, Hannes had me on her lap holding me close. They asked me whether I wanted to keep coming to the farm? If I did, which I liked so much, the milk delivery run mainly — I was "never ever" to tell a soul what had happened to me that lunch time, especially my father or mother. This, she said, was only to be known by the four of us — and I was always to be in sight of any of the *three of them at all times*, and several small chores which I carried out, such as collecting the eggs from the hay loft were to cease. So, I only saw him when we took the horse out delivering the milk. I kept my secret sixty years.

However, at that time capital punishment was the law. If someone were to take another person's life, they would be hung by the neck until they died. Had my father known what David Williams did to me, he would have killed him, and this would have broken up our happy family, and the three daughters on the farm knew this. Several times when we were together they questioned me as to our secret which was to be ours forever. But I cried many times too, whenever it came to my mind and it often did; the tears ran down my cheeks and I couldn't stop crying, until I felt exhausted. Whether he was punished, by the farmer I never knew. Perhaps the sisters did keep it to themselves.

Then one day, they bought a new horse. He was a young beautiful horse, although not placid in any way. He was highly strung and appeared nervous at the least sound. His ears would "stand up" and he was not at ease. His whole body would tense up, as if he feared something. "Not the type of horse for a milk float," I heard the men say. A delivery horse had to be of a calm and placid nature. One you could rely upon. This horse was named "Bullet" and against all opposition Ceinwen took him out in the milk float on his first journey to Trebanos. He trotted quicker than the old faithful, and on our return home, we three got off the float, and before the lad could open the farmyard gate, Bullet jumped it and got stuck one side of the gate and the float the other. Fortunately my dad was close at hand and he dismantled the float, at the same time, calming the horse. Dad was wonderful with horses, and his advice was "This horse is too fast and nervous for a milk float, especially as the milk round is on the main road." So Ceinwen was told she should carry on deliveries with the old placid carthorse. Margaretta was far more dependable than Ceinwen and she too felt Bullet was trouble.

Everything went back to normal for a while and my days on the farm were deliriously happy, and how my summer school holidays flew by; until the next holiday.

Ceinwen begged to be able to take Bullet that day in the float, against all opposition she got her wish, and we were away. I believe she had made plans before we left, as she decided as we trotted along, that she would reverse our regular routine and deliver first to the houses in the wooded copse, called "Glanrhyd", which would normally be the last call before returning to the farm. It was a beautiful place to live, and I often walked the "driveway" with them, to deliver the milk. This day however, Ceinwen and the lad, David, carried the milk cans and I was left in the float, unattended. That was all I remembered of that morning, until I awoke two miles further down the road, sitting in someone's parlour, with the young doctor in attendance. He had recently moved into the "practice". The horse, it was understood, had been frightened by a rabbit and had taken off at speed, only to topple on rounding a bend in the road, outside "All Saints Church", Pontardawe, and ending up outside one of the four cottages near the church named "Primrose Row". I must have been unconscious several hours, as the first person I saw, among many faces, when I regained consciousness, was my mam, standing there looking at me. She was wearing her crossover pinafore and held a black-lead brush in her hand. David, the lad, had run back to my mam and also to the farm, and told them what had happened. When mam got the news of the accident, she was cleaning the kitchen range and had run more than two miles from the hillside to the village, to get to me. The doctor came from his nearby surgery in the Uplands, when told of the accident by one of the ladies living in Primrose Row Cottages. He was trimming the tips of my fingers, after removing all the dirt and gravel from them; as I regained consciousness. My left leg was heavily bandaged, from knee to ankle. My nose wore a large plaster, and my head had been plugged in several places then stitched, where I had been badly cut from the milk bottles, which the farm was changing over to. "Cut to $1/8$" of the brain," the doctor told Mam. "A very lucky little girl."

Things could have been worse. I was alive. As the three ladies from the cottages said, they did not know there was a child under the horse. The horse tried several times to raise himself up and each time he screamed in agony; it was then, that these ladies stepped back and away from the horse, in fear, and got a shock. There was a small child under the horse and the horse had the shaft of the milk float through his side.

I was wearing a green "French beret" that day and the doctor told Mam, "That beret saved her from severe brain damage." My uncle, Daniel, gave me the beret, after swapping his at a football match; Wales v Ireland.

There were no X-rays in those days, but I did get severe pain in both shoulders, if I raised my arms up. Eventually it was found I had two broken shoulders; identical fractures; also a broken coccyx.

Ceinwen was almost reaching the milk float when the horse bolted. She threw the churn and ran. She just managed to grab the handrail at the back of the float, but no doubt she thought possibly she could get on the step and grab the reins, and bring Bullet to a halt. She was dragged the whole way and had severe injuries also. Her ankle bone was worn away from contact with the road, and her nose was broken. The horse was badly hurt, and at first it was thought he would have to be shot. The shaft of the float was through his side, but the doctor was able to attend to the horse and he recovered.

By then I had lost consciousness again, and found myself back at the farm in Grandma's feather bed. The doctor had asked my mother's permission for both patients to be under one roof, making it easier for him to treat us and see to our recovery.

Ceinwen, had planned the change of pattern that day, by starting at Glanrhyd and continuing deliveries on the way to Trebanos, in order to have a "straight run back from Trebanos", giving the horse his head to see what speed he could do. Really, she was responsible for this serious accident, as she would not listen to the family. I myself owe my life to the ladies in Primrose Row Cottages.

I had been recuperating at the farm for several weeks, and feeling stronger, but I now longed to be home with my Mam and Dad, and so it was arranged for me to go home, where a nurse would call daily to dress my wounds. The side of my left leg was badly cut and the rather large wound at my knee hurt from the iodine which went into it. I dreaded the daily visit. I would cry before she unrolled my bandages, knowing what was to come.

Most of my days, whilst immobile, I sat in a small pushchair, at the side of the house, with the footrest extended, and Mam would pop out to make sure I wasn't in the boiling sun, move me if I was, then dash back indoors to continue her busy chores, looking to my baby sister, who still ailed from time to time, and to cook the meals. My sister, Mary, spent most of her time indoors. We were never close friends. She was almost two years older than me. We were different personalities, and we clashed when together. She liked doing needlework but she would not do the chores. My dad would say I was "The one who has to learn the hard way," and Mary was the "Lady of the House."

Whenever visitors came long distances to see us, mainly from the Gower, Mary was asked to do her "party piece" and soberly, she would ask for complete silence, whilst someone else would oblige by fetching her a chair. On this she stood and recited "The Owl and the Pussycat". I don't remember her ever completing it, as I would go into fits of laughter, and she would refuse to start again, but at the first chance of catching me on my own, she would give me a hard slap on my face! And the slaps did hurt!

Whilst I was convalescing at my home, two senior boys from Trebanos School, called at our house and told Mam, they had been sent by Mr Williams the Headmaster, to ask whether I would like to come down to school for the afternoon, and sit next to my friend Beryl Williams. I did — the boys crossed their hands together, I sat on them, and hung around their necks, and we got to school.

Beryl was admitted to Gellyneath Isolation Hospital on the Sunday with diptheria — I followed on the Monday — still in bandages, on head, nose and leg! Two more pupils in our class, another girl and a boy were admitted — his mother was allowed to sit next to him (in mask and sterile clothes) but sadly he died. I knew him and his two sisters.

After three to four weeks, we were allowed to go out into the grounds for fresh air, having got over the critical days. Visitors climbed up small permanent ladders to see us through the windows, and Mam and Dad would show me what they had brought me. Biscuits normally.

The day came, when I was ready to leave the Isolation Hospital, and after I had taken a bath, a nurse washed my hair, then told me to kneel in front of a large open fire and threatened me, if I dared move. She then left the room. As I was particularly frightened of this nurse, I grew hotter and hotter, by the time she came back, I had a nasty scorch mark on my neck in the bargain.

My dad was waiting in the hall when she brought me out ready for home, and together we walked slowly, calling in my granfer's house on the way, where they gave me a basket of fresh fruit, and fussed over me.

In the meantime, my dad was still out of work and walking from farm to farm, looking for a day's labour. There were other farms further over the mountain past "Pen-y-Graig" Farm. The furthest was known as "The Allt", "Alltyvanog" and these people were strangers to us. Dad got offered a few weeks' work there, when "Pen-y-Graig" was slack and on recommendation, also, he was quite happy to walk the extra distance there and back daily. By the end of the week, he was asked by the farmer's wife to bring his family to dinner one evening.

Although Mam, was always at home, we did accept the kind invitation and arrived for dinner, walking all the way with Enid on Dad's shoulders. She did not weigh much and was a tiny child. I, by now, had recovered from my accident.

We had taken our places for dinner, when in came cook, sporting a large "pinny" and "frilled cap" and carrying an enormous goose on a tray. I cringed. It had its head on! I cannot remember eating any of it, but raspberries and fresh cream followed and after dinner, they were chatting to Mam and fussed over us. They were extremely kind and showed great respect for our dad, and they made us very welcome.

As we had a long walk downhill to school, Mam packed us sandwiches and made a can of cocoa. The cocoa we were allowed to place near the hob in the teachers' study, upstairs, and lunch time we would fetch it and have our lunch at our desks. There were no "School Dinners" at our Elementary School. My sister Mary and I, were the only children allowed in the classroom in the lunch time. Once we had eaten our lunch, we had to go out into the yard.

I enjoyed my school days. I made many friends and I behaved myself in class. There was only one time when I was sent out into the hall to see the headmaster, which normally meant "the cane". It was during Needlework class and I had been eating sweets, licking my fingers, then, proceeding with my sewing, when the teacher called me out to inspect my work. She found my needle so sticky and it was not the first time I had been warned, I was sent out into the Hall. I never got caned, but I returned to my class after the headmaster had left the Hall for his Study, and I think the teacher was more upset than I was. I had only been given a "ticking off". She thought I had been caned and she was full of remorse. 'Serve her right' I thought. I let her think she had got me caned! I never did like sewing!

Whilst at the Elementary School, my dad was feeling ill one morning. He got up and shaved, said he had a "sore throat". He had something at the back of his throat, like a "pea". Once he saw our doctor, he was sent eight miles to Swansea Hospital, where they sprayed his throat, and with an "appliance" clipped off the offending "pea". He was told to gargle for a few days, and informed they had removed a tumour from the back of his throat. It never returned or troubled him again.

My days on the farm, became few and far between after my accident. Many of my school friends I saw during school holidays. Mam would include them at meal times. Her life consisted of baking and sewing. We were always nicely dressed and were well fed; there being a continual supply of freshly baked bread, currant loaf and a huge tin of bread pudding. If we were hungry at any time, we helped ourselves, until our main meal.

Gwyneth Thomas, was one of my friends and lived just beyond "Pen-y-Graig Farm", on a "smallholding", called "The Spa". She was a bigger girl than I was, and full of fun. The shaded lane with the running stream which I loved, because of the beauty of the bluebells and violets, was a short cut from our house to her grandparents' farm, known as "Tyn-y-Pant" and some days I joined her at the farm during the holidays. She helped around the farm, feeding the animals and milking the cows or, when her granddad, who was a dear old man, with "specs" on the end of his nose, was also milking, she would play tricks on him all the time — especially if he was milking the next cow to her. She would call out "Granddad" and as his head popped out she would squirt him in his eye with milk from the cow's udder!

As our garden was higher than the house, there were steps up to the garden, which was always cultivated with plenty of vegetables. Dad planted rows and rows of peas, and whenever my younger sister Enid disappeared for a while, we always knew where to find her. She would be among the rows, opening the pods and eating the peas! She would leave the pods on the stalks!

One day, Mam asked me to walk the Tarmac Road, and go to the village of Pontardawe to give an order at the Corn Stores for chicken food to be delivered; this was the same road where my accident happened. I was now about nine years of age. As it was a nice sunny day, she added, "You may take Enid" who was then about four or five years old, and "Don't rush. Go slowly so that Enid can get the benefit of a change of scenery and don't get her short of breath." We ambled along, and got to the shop, which stood at that time on the left-hand side of the road, just before the crossroads, practically on the bridge over the river. Suddenly, as we waited to be served, a policeman ran into the store and asked, "Has anyone got a small brown and white terrier, as he has just been killed by the traffic?" We joined the little crowd which had gathered, and recognised Paddy. We howled and said he was ours, although we never knew he was following us as we did not look back when we made the journey to the village. As both Enid and I cried, someone picked Paddy up and dropped him into the river below, which was terrible; he should have been collected later and Dad would have buried him in the garden. When we got home, red-eyed and tired, we told Mam Paddy was dead. Poor Paddy, he had a very short life. David Williams later recovered Paddy's collar and gave it to us.

Not long after losing Paddy, my dad was in the village of Pontardawe, which was the main village with all kinds of stores, also, where he had to go each week for his £1.9s.0d dole money. He was passing the fish shop (wet) when Mr Jones said "Hello Denis, can you help me?"
    My dad said "Yes, as long as it's not money!"

"No Denis, it's about a home for a dog. He's an Airedale breed, and he only has sight in one eye. A beautiful dog — and I think he will have a better life up on the hillside than with us in the shop."

Actually the dog had bitten a customer and he had been told to "Get rid of it". And so Dad arrived home with this dog on a piece of string. He was a golden and black colour and his name was "Sykee". Dad made a kennel for the dog, should he be left alone. During the daytime he was on a long lead in the kennel, whilst Dad was on the farm, and let off as soon as Dad got home.

Now, our house was one of a pair of new houses, detached, and our neighbours had a small Pekinese dog. It used to come into our garden in the daytime and annoy Sykee by coming so far, and with its hind legs would scratch earth into our dog's face, but as soon as Dad let Sykee off the lead, he would jump over the dividing wall and grab this little dog, like a duster, and after shaking it several times, he would throw it up in the air and it would land in its own back garden. This went on day after day, but still the Pekinese came back for more!

The neighbours in the house were very nice — they had two girls, Annie and Betty Nutt. In the kindest of words we used to say they also had a "Nutty" dog! We were all invited in for a musical evening one week and it was most enjoyable. They had a xylophone and the father could play it well; in fact, he was most accomplished.

Later, that evening, when we crossed over to our house next door, Mam said "Good God! Someone has broken into our house whilst we were next door." We found Mam's youngest brother Daniel and his fiancée Sarah, sitting there, having demolished most of her "bread pudding"!! He had managed to open a small window to get in. I'm surprised Sykee let them in, as he was indoors evenings to mornings.

All Mam's brothers were in full employment, also Sarah, but they were not generous to us in any way.

Our neighbours' house, being next to the cliff face of "Pen-y-Graig Farm", one of its field came to the top of the rock. I stood one day, watching from our house; I was hypnotised, one of their cows had broken through the fence at the top of the cliff, and there was not enough time to warn the farmer. I saw it get nearer and nearer to the edge, then it fell, all the way, bellowing as it fell, until it reached the bottom at the side of their house. I was not allowed to go and see it, but it was dead and its horns had been ripped off.

There were many houses down the lane from us. We were isolated, being near the shelter of the hillside; but it was nicer in every way. A boy named Ernest lived in one of them; actually it was a bungalow. His parents were quite old, compared to ours, and they were always beating him. My mam used to say, they were cruel. She said "The world will beat him enough when he grows up!" He was always late for school, having to do lots of jobs at home before he left, and of course when he got to school he would get the cane for being late! Poor Ernest, he could not win; his was a hard life.

Out of the £1.9s.0d (£1.45) Mam had each week, she paid 9s rent and gave Dad 1s to go for a pint of beer on Saturday evenings. He would go and play skittles in the village pub in Trebanos, and if he won, he had his pint and Mam shared a bar of Fry's cream chocolate with us!

On his way home, taking the rough pathway, opposite the empty "haunted house"; an old house smothered in growth, there was a small bungalow hidden by trees and shrubs, it was difficult to see the bungalow. Dad told us he used to say "Good Evening" to the old man leaning on the gate as he walked past. The old man was always smoking a pipe and he had a white beard.

Now, we knew as children, no old man occupied that bungalow. A young family with two little boys lived there and the little boys both had bow legs, as did their father. So after arguing with us over this, he made enquiries and was told that the old man he had described, used to live in the bungalow years before and had long since died? Mam preferred to think Dad had had a drop too much! But he would retort laughingly "What, on a shilling!".

The occasional Saturday evening, when my father went for a pint to Pontardawe, he would return home on the Tarmac Road, past "All Saints Church" Glanrhyd and Tyn-y-Pant Farm, then along the narrower road below "Pen-y-Graig Farm" to our house. There was talk at times of someone on the Tarmac Road, later at night, holding up folk going home. Even on a moonlight night, parts of the road were thickly wooded and in darkness. It was on such a night, my father was coming home, a bag of small swedes under one arm, when out of the trees stepped a masked man, his hat pulled well down over his forehead. He asked my father "Have you got a light?" My father moved the bag of swedes to his left armpit, and as he put his right hand deep into his pocket the man said "Stick 'em up." Dad lost no time but swung his fist so fast, it caught the man just near "the cheekbone" and the man fell to his knees; however, he was up immediately and ran into the woods.

We were up late that night, Mam and me, and Dad's face was deathly white when he came into the house. He related what had happened to him and how he knew from the force of the blow he struck, that the man's face would carry bruising; and even more so, he was one hundred per cent positive, who the man was.

Mam said "Why didn't you hit him with the bag of swedes?"

He said "No, we want them for dinner tomorrow!" Mam begged him not to go out again, but Dad said "I'm going down to the police station in the village and report the assault."

This he did and the police inspector phoned colleagues in the police station at Pontardawe, to say if anyone called to report an assault, he was to be detained, as he could believe one hundred per cent what my dad had told him.

We waited to hear what else he had to say, before going to bed. He said, "This man, who I'm positive of, has a bitch who has just given birth to some lovely puppies. So tomorrow I'm going to pay him a visit, look at the puppies, show an interest in maybe buying one. I shall see if his face is bruised."

This he did, and sure enough, the man's cheekbone area was badly bruised. The man, came from a respected family, and being local, would have known every inch of the Tarmac Road. And so, against Mam's advice, Dad arranged to go with a friend and watch the road, one dark evening; but as they waited, they saw an elderly lady walking home, and fearing they would scare her, they walked on ahead, but heard footsteps running away into the wood.

Whilst I was still at Junior School, we were taught Domestic Science. On the days we were cooking, we used to take all the ingredients to the school further up the road, which was a lot nearer home; and so, on those days I went home to lunch.

This school was divided into two sections; Cookery and Woodwork. The playground was also divided. I loved cooking, and I had a boyfriend whom I thought was lovely. He had thick curly hair and blue eyes and his name was Lewis Lewis. He was in my class at the Elementary School and did Woodwork the same day as I did Cookery. I used to pass him some of my warm cakes through the railings in the break.

The kitchen where we worked was enormous, with rows of clean scrubbed wooden tables. Two girls worked to each table and we listened to the cookery mistress eagerly, as we followed her instructions step by step, wondering whether the recipe would turn out as good as hers did. We need not have worried, it was always delicious. I found all the girls were keen on cooking, and even the clearing away and washing-up was done willingly. We were always given the recipe for the following week to copy from the blackboard before we left for home. One day, we had to make a bread and butter pudding and Mam put all the ingredients, plus the earthenware dish, in a patchwork leather bag.

The pudding turned out a treat, but when I came to take it home for lunch, it was pouring with rain, so I slid it sideways into the bag, keeping it upright and hurried home with it. Mam had lunch ready that day as she usually did when I was at the cookery class, but when she took the pudding out of the leather bag, it was a mass of different colours, from the wet leather. I was soaked too, but bad weather never bothered me, I was happiest out of doors and if my hair got wet — it curled!!

I was now growing older and my sister Mary had left the Junior School and was travelling six miles by train from Pontardawe Station to the Grammar School at Ystalyfera (IYS). We never had much in common when we were children. She liked to sew nice things and embroider. My days on the farm grew less after I had the accident with the horse and milk float.

By the time I was eleven, I too had passed into the Grammar School at Ystalyfera, and before I began my studies there, the good news at last, after five and a half years unemployed, Dad had word from the steelworks saying there was work for him again as a boilerman. Mam and Dad were both elated. *Dad started work* and was so happy now to be earning a living wage again. He worked shiftwork 10 p.m. — 6 a.m., 6 a.m. — 2 p.m. and 2 p.m. — 10 p.m. Occasionally when he did the afternoon shift 2 p.m. — 10 p.m., if his relief did not arrive at 10 p.m. he would have to work on through the night until the morning relief came at 6 a.m. There was no way in which Dad could let Mam know when he was "working on", so she would wait a while after the time he normally arrived home, then she would prepare sandwiches and a can of tea.

On these occasions, she would send me down the hill to the steelworks with it. It would be quite dark and I shudder now when I think of a child of nearly eleven years, being out at that time of night. Mary never went, she was a strong-willed child.

Now, to get to the works, I had to reach the main road through the Cwm at the bottom of the hill and walk through to the village of Pontardawe. Before reaching the "turn off" leading to the works, there was a short road named "The Black Road", but to get to it, there was "The Avenue". Extremely tall trees lined the sides of the road here and overhung; it was always pitch-black, ghostly. You could not see the sky when walking through The Avenue, and I was terrified, especially if an owl hooted! So I found another way of getting to the works without going through The Avenue. It was before reaching it, on the main road opposite Derw Road; there was an "opening", a stile which took you down to the canal, and by feeling my way across "The Lock Gates", I found myself in the works. I could so easily have slipped and fallen into the canal of course, and Mam would have been puzzled how I came to be in there if I had drowned, which I most certainly would have, had I fallen in, and it gives me "goose pimples" when I think of it.

Returning home, Dad would see me to the Black Road the same road which was the Bridge Road over the canal and then I *had* to return through "The Avenue" to get home. I did that trip a few times. I can never remember my elder sister ever doing it. (Possibly because she slept with my younger sister Enid).

Of course, I had chores to do at home, mostly running errands, washing dishes, dusting, but once done, time was my own. Although I was expected to do a certain amount of reading from the books Mam had got for us. She used to "cut tokens" from the newspapers and send away for the books. I remember two cupboards in the parlour, one on either side of the fireplace, full of books, encyclopaedias, dictionaries, and the complete works of Charles Dickens. Other books contained "Fable Stories" and I used to get enthralled reading them. I'm sure this reading helped me to get good results in English at school.

All the years we lived on "The Graig"; six years; we had a regular visitor. He was an old man with long hair — a pedlar man. We were always pleased to see him, and I would run indoors and tell Mam he was coming. She always bought a "little something" from him. He would sit on the grass outside our front door, have a glass of Mam's lemon drink and open the box to reveal a collection of accessories for sewing. His name was Francis.

'Francis'

Old Francis was a Pedlar Man, he walked the country lanes;
He wore a long grey mackintosh and always looked the same.
The hat he wore upon his head, had lost its shape years gone —
His face, it never altered much, his hair — it was quite long.
Upon his back, he had a box, it held 'most everything,
Like cottons, lace and ribbons, and some thread and safety pins.
Although the months grew far between — the visits which he made,
He always was a welcome sight, as he plodded up "The Lane".
He'd reach the top and out of breath, he'd sit and rest awhile,
And after some refreshment — there was this "gentle smile".
We never knew, from whence he came, a 'tramp' some people called him.
We thought he was a gentleman, bearing what fate had dealt him.
We'd wave goodbye and wait until he'd disappeared from view,
Where his travels took him to, well that we never knew.

Mam was a great cook and our house had the beautiful aroma of warm yeast and flour. She made six loaves at one time plus, currant bread, and kept it in a huge earthenware pan covered with a large folded sheet. She was also superstitious. If she saw any soot flapping on the bars of the fire, then we were due for visitors and coincidence or not, somebody would call on us. A thunderstorm saw her run and cover all the mirrors, put the cutlery away and she even took the hairpins from her hair. She wore her hair in a "rounded bun" at the back of her head. I continued with the same superstition. I was sure I would get struck by lightning, if I left hairgrips in my hair.

Her days were kept busy sewing and knitting socks for Dad. She used to send me to the next village of Pontardawe to Scales the Drapers, to get samples of dress materials for us to have a new dress each. The assistant was a local girl and knew my mam, so I would return home with little snippings of materials, pinned to a piece of paper, showing the price per yard; i.e. 9d, 1s and the best 1s.3d a yard (4½p, 6p, and 7½p). Mam would examine the snippings and tell us we could choose any pattern from a particular range, so we knew we would like the dress when it was finished. Mine always had a "little collar, edged in lace", puff sleeves and waisted, because I was a tall girl, I had a long neck, and my mother would cheer me up, or try to, by saying, a long neck is elegant, look at a swan!! She always had us looking nice. She never thought of herself ever. She was proud of us.

Not all was serene and quiet on the hillside. There was terrible news one day, of a young lad, around seven years of age, from our Junior School who was playing on some waste ground near the playing fields in Trebanos, when he was chased by an older boy who was subnormal, a teenager. The little boy panicked and climbed some very high railings to escape his assailant, only to find he had landed on the sewage tank, and probably thinking the crust on the top of the tank was concrete, ran across it and of course he drowned. The teenager's family were butchers; the son never attended school.

The hooter in the works would always be sounded if there was an accident, and Dad told us one day of two sisters who worked together in the works. They wore heavy clog-type boots, and around six o'clock one morning, at the start of their shift, one of the sisters slipped, and fell into a vat of acid. Another younger man, one evening, got his leg caught in a flywheel and lost his leg. We would listen in awe, but Mam would sit down and cry for them as she knew most of these families.

A regular occurrence each year, at the Elementary School on St David's Day, was that everyone either wore a daffodil on one's chest, or a leek, made of linen — white on bottom and green on top. Some of the children wore the "Welsh costume"; it was very attractive, especially the lace collars and the large black hat edged under the brim in white lace. Midway through the morning, Mrs Williams, a local JP, and whose family business was a bakery by the name of "Blackmores", would come along to the school and share out tins of ginger biscuits to the children in the yard. We were also given an orange. This was a regular occurrence whilst I was at the Junior School; then school was over for the day.

I remember also, a couple of brothers who were in a higher class than I was, and one of them was being constantly caned by the teacher in that class. Now caning was carried out by the headmaster only. If a pupil was unruly and misbehaved, he was told to go and stand in the Assembly Hall, and at various intervals, the headmaster would come downstairs from his study and deal with the disobedient pupil. Most times a warning was meted out, but other times — it was the cane. But we were all aware, that when you reached this particular class in the school, this teacher was a "dab hand" at doling out the cane, to boys only; then he hid the cane behind the blackboard!

This young lad, had been having more than his fair share of punishment and one day, during "lunch time" there was a disturbance in the school yard between the two brothers. They only lived a "stone's throw" away from school, so there was no reason for them to be loitering in the yard, by pretending to be fighting. Sure enough, this teacher came out. He was a short, small man, with dark oiled black hair combed closely to his head, and his black gown blowing around his ankles. (My sister and I were the only two in the dividing yard as we stayed for lunch). We watched, anxiously, when suddenly, on the top of the wall appeared the older brothers of the two boys, who had long left school. They leaned down and hoisted this teacher over the wall onto some waste ground the other side, and when they had finished with him, he was a sorry sight. He never caned their brothers again, and as far as I knew, nothing was done about the assault.

We have all heard the story of Jekyll and Hyde. This same teacher was the church organist at a local church in the next village of Pontardawe. Outside the school gates he was a very pleasant person. No one would have thought he could have been so cruel.

During the summer holidays, Mam's cousin, Nellie, would come up from Waunarllwydd, near Gowerton, for the day, with her two daughters, Emmie and Dulcie, who were about the same age as Mary and myself. I was sometimes allowed to go back with them on the Swansea train for two weeks. I looked forward to it and enjoyed every minute; then Mam would come and collect me. She always emphasized I had the "Wanderer or Gypsy" spirit in me, but I believe, the "middle child" in a family of three children loses her status when a new baby arrives on the scene and so, is given, more freedom than is normal.

Going back some years, Mam told us that several of her relatives were lost at sea. They were members of the Mumbles' lifeboat team. Their name was Gammon, and she said, two or three from the same family were lost in the same rescue calls.

I understand a poem was later written about "The Women off Mumbles Head", who were supposed to have formed a lifeline by joining hands and going into the sea to help to rescue the men. Recently (1996), two more lifeboat men of that family were lost at sea. I loved to hear of relatives long gone, what kind of lives they led; but not all the tales were happy ones. Mam remembers, as a small girl herself, going into Swansea with a great-aunt who would "pay in" gold sovereigns at the bank. She must have been fairly wealthy. I don't know who she bequeathed it to. Our family did not see any of it!

Summer holidays also meant blackberrying. We were sent out with paper-lined baskets, which we filled and brought home. We chose the fruit at its best, and after Mam had checked it through and cleaned it, she boiled the fruit with sugar and made blackberry jelly which was then given to the convent in the next village, where there was an orphanage. Usually, the younger priest would visit and take a basketful of jars of jelly preserve.

Dad was a Catholic of course and he normally took Mary and myself to the church in Clydach on Sunday mornings, where Mary would be regularly sick as soon as the incense was dispersed! My delight in going, was to listen to the nuns' chorus. They had beautiful sweet voices. We could not see them; they were behind us in a separate part of the church. How pure their voices were.

My mother, did not change her religion, but agreed to bring children up in the Catholic faith. When Mary was a baby, our Irish grandmother, visiting us, on finding out the baby had not been christened, waited until the time arrived, when no one was around; picked up Mary and taking the footpath along the canal to the next village, she had her christened in their faith.

It was meant that I too should also be christened in the Catholic faith, but the elder priest, who was to confirm his younger congregation, had a dispute with Dad, over not confirming Mary as she did not know all her Catechism by heart, although several illiterate children were to be allowed confirmation. We stopped going to church, and when Dad turned up without us, the old priest told him "You are banned from Communion until you bring your family back to the faith." Dad walked out, and changed to the Church of England faith and became a Protestant. Then before my Confirmation, I was "Christened" in St Peter's Church, Pontardawe. I was eleven years of age, with my aunt, Elizabeth, (Mam's sister) and her

My Irish grandmother — Mrs Annie Healy

*My Welsh grandfather — Mr Arthur Richards
with Bobby Grant and Geofrey Richards*

My mother Mary with sister and I   *Mary and I in our Sunday best*

The author in Ystalyfera Grammar School uniform with young sister Enid, taken at Raglan House, Coedcae

My mother and father at Raglan House, Coedcae

My uncle — Michael Healy — Royal Munster Fusiliers

A friend laying a wreath from the family — on his grave

Michael Healy's grave in France

The medals won by Michael Healy, including the Military Medal and Bar, the Distinguished Conduct Medal and the Albert Medal

The author top of the tree, with sister Mary below

The author, when preparing to join the Air Ministry

husband, Uncle James, being my godparents.

Aunt and Uncle, they too lived at the top of a hill, in the village of Clydach. It was quiet and peaceful; all the houses clung to one side of the hill, with green banks on the other side. I understand that from the height where they lived, one could see Swansea, five or six miles away. Both were chapel members. Uncle James was a deacon and Aunt Elizabeth a deaconess. Aunt Elizabeth, had been a nanny most of her life to a family living at "Bryneithin", The Uplands, Pontardawe.

Aunt Elizabeth married late in life. She was an attractive lady; full featured, dark hair framing her face. Mam was taller, very slim and wore her hair plaited, then rolled into a "bun" at the nape of her neck. Aunt Elizabeth presented me with a beautiful ivory prayer book after my christening. The vicar, having dipped his finger into the water, made the sign of the cross on my forehead. I was past ten and a half years of age.

Chapter Four

It was whilst Dad was back working at the steelworks, that he was talking to an older gentleman who he had worked with some years before, and the older gentleman told Dad that he was planning to leave the steelworks to keep a "smallholding" in another village, and did Dad know anyone who would buy his house? Dad said he did not, and thought no more about it, until one day, the old gentleman spoke again about getting a buyer for his house. He told Dad that he would like to see him and his family living there, and he was prepared to let Dad have the house at a bargain price if only he would consider it. Dad said he would talk things over with Mam, as Dad had no money, being out of work for six years; but the gentleman even knew how Dad could get his mortgage, so determined was he to see us settled into his house. Mam was delighted and felt their luck was changing at last, and so we moved from The Graig, Trebanos to "Raglan House", Coedcae, Pontardawe and I commenced my school in Ystalyfera Grammar.

Again, this stone house was nestled to a hillside, called "The Barley", with a "right of way" footpath to the hillside. It was a large house; four bedrooms, three rooms downstairs, one very large, a pantry, and a large outhouse where one did the daily chores, a coal house also, plus an outside flush toilet. Leading from the back of the house was the first garden, with apple trees and plum trees and a vegetable plot. Further on was a couple of pigsties and chicken houses; even a shed for a horse. Then on a lower level, a large plot of land separating our house from the neighbours next door. This garden was protected by a very high laurel hedge. Currant bushes, red, black and white, several variegated holly trees, herbs of different types, and the laurel hedge continued from the neighbours up to the entrance of our house. A front entrance to the house also had a laurel hedge showing above the wall; it was a small frontage and each side had an hydrangea bush. Under the windows of the double-fronted house, were thick beds of lilies of the valley.

I was eleven at the time, and from here I started my studies at the Grammar School of Ystalyfera (IYS) with Mary, although she never walked beside me. The house was known as "Raglan House", Coedcae. The old gentleman had been employed at Raglan Castle many years before and named his house after it. Dad soon built a bathroom and toilet behind the kitchen.

Mam decided, that whilst Dad worked in the steelworks, she would run the "smallholding" and so we started off with chickens and a couple of small pigs in the sty, as done by the previous owner.

The house was made of stone and the walls were eighteen inches thick. The pantry which was big, had a window one side; half-glass and half-mesh. Mam stored the shelves along the side with jars of preserves, bottles of pickled onions, chutneys and other "home-made" goodies. There was also a huge "stone slab" where they had salted the pigs. This had been in use for many years, for the salt had spread into the wall which divided the pantry and the parlour. We found, that, no matter how many times the parlour was papered, salt bubbles formed on the newly-dried paper, after a while. So one week, some years later, they decided they would keep no more pigs. Dad decided to knock down the wall and build another with new bricks. That solved the problem for future decorating.

In the kitchen, we hung the pig's meat. We had gammons and sides of bacon hanging from huge hooks in the ceiling; so we had a regular cooked breakfast each morning. When a pig was to be killed, it would have reached a certain weight, and one of us would walk the ten minutes to the village of Ynismeudw (it bordered Pontardawe), and ask the butcher when could he call. It was usually during school holidays. The day would arrive, and we children would be sent out with a packet of sandwiches and some drinks for a couple of hours. By the time we returned, the pig would be shaved clean and hanging pegged out from a hook in the ceiling and a lot of local women would be helping to clean the inside of the pig and making faggots. They were made from belly pork, liver, onions, breadcrumbs, sage, and each one, wrapped in a piece of fry (suet skin), placed in large meat tins and baked. Mam would share these tins of faggots with the women who had helped to clean the inside of the pig, and there would be a rush in the afternoon when local lads would try to get to the house first, for the bladder, which they used as a football!!

The kitchen/dining room was already papered in a thick colourful paper, with birds on it. Two large pictures hung on the wall, facing the door; my grandmother who died in childbirth, and the other one was Dad's brother Michael, who was killed in the Great War, aged twenty-five years. A grandmother clock sat importantly between the two pictures. On each end of the mantelpiece stood a large amber lion, and some pretty ornaments in the middle. Higher up each side of the mantelpiece was a nice roomy cupboard where Mam kept private documents, insurance books, etc. When the insurance man called, if Mam had her hands full of washing or baking — he knew where to get the books, would bring them "up to date" — put the money in his bag and return the insurance books to the cupboard. A large wooden wireless with a fretwork front panel, sat on the windowsill. Another large mirror hung on the wall between the window and the back door, and we girls would have a last look in it before we left the house for school or to go anywhere. If we patronised it too much, Dad would remark "Why don't you hang that mirror around your neck and go, if you're going!" He would tell us not to be vain!

Outside the back door, there was a slabbed patio. There was a buddleia tree and a laburnum tree, and umpteen arches of roses everywhere. Below the wall was the second garden with fruit bushes. It was very pretty, and a happy house my mam said, when she saw it. She was told by the old gentleman, the buddleia tree was planted to keep the devil out, and the laburnum to keep the gypsies out. It never did!

It was the top house on the right-hand side of Coedcae. The "right of way" lane around the side of the house, next to The Barley also took you to the golf course and the old church of Llanquicke. It was not as lonely here as it was on "The Graig", as there was always someone passing by, who would look over the garden wall and pass the time of day.

Llanquicke Church was the "mother" church. There were three others in the village; St Peter's, St Mary's and All Saints. On special days, the service would be held at Llanquicke and many people would pass by on their way to church. It was rather creepy up at the "mother" church, and I can remember being shown a tree around the back of the church, where someone hung himself.

The laburnum tree never kept the gypsies away; they were regular callers in the summer months. Mam would let the gypsies sit on the back doorstep and rest, or feed their babies. I know she was superstitious in believing they could "put a curse" on her, so she never sent them packing!

The flagstones outside the back door were not evenly laid and one day Mam was leaving the kitchen to go round to the wash house when she saw the cat on the doorstep, hitting out at something. She took a closer look and found it was a fat snake, about four feet long, and it was coming towards the door. She pulled the door closed and called to our neighbour for help — she was terrified of snakes — and the neighbour came, carrying a big iron bar. "Get some boiling water quickly," he said as the snake disappeared under one of the flagstones. Mam grabbed a kettle from the hob, kicked the cat out of the way and poured the boiling water under the flagstone she thought it might be under. Sure enough, out came the snake quickly, only to be killed with the iron bar. The memory of this never fades, as the snake was thrown over the garden wall, but instead, it got caught on the overhanging branch of a tree in the garden, and hung there! After a week, all that was left was the skin; the birds had had a feast. There were many snakes around the hillside, and they terrified me, and still do.

The water butt at the side of the house held rainwater which we used, to wash our hair.

Dad was now progressing in the steelworks and things were looking up.

I had commenced my new studies in the Grammar School with Mary and we both left home early in the morning to walk the fifteen minutes to the station to catch the train. I was happy at my school. I took to most subjects except History and Geography. Sewing too, I was useless at. I always gained high marks in English, Welsh, Latin, French, Chemistry and Maths (Arithmetic, Algebra and Geometry) and when I look back at my School Reports, these subjects saw me many times "top of my class". I remember my teachers, who were all very nice.

When I first commenced school at the IYS, our headmistress, Miss Lloyd, was French by birth and also our French teacher. One morning she asked all new girls to stay behind in the Assembly Hall. Once all the other students had left, we were asked to sing once more, the morning's hymn. She passed behind each girl and listened. I stopped singing, but she "poked" me and said "Sing on", then told me to stay behind in the Assembly Hall. When she had completed her task, I found quite a few students standing aside, as there were three classes to each year. We were then told we were to be trained for the well-known school choir, and naturally, as older students completed their studies and left school, others moved up in the choir and we replaced from the lower section.

Oh, what a joy I had to come! I had been chosen to be one of the school's choir girls, who were well known as an extremely good choir in the valley. Summertime, we would present a Choral Recital, once a month. We travelled from Ystalyfera up the valley. Normally any girl living in the village we were to perform in, was asked whether her family would kindly feed us and sleep us overnight when we would return to school the following day. We held our recitals in chapels and we always stood up in the balcony and commenced our evening's recital with "Jesu Joy of Man's Desire", and the chapel was full to capacity each time.

These new friends I met mainly at school. Back in the village, six miles or more, I still had my friends from the Elementary School and we met up at the weekends.

Just after I started my new school at Ystalyvera, I came home one afternoon; I was so grown up now at eleven years of age. I did not change my school uniform, but I asked Mam's permission to go to the village for about one hour. She agreed, on condition I was back within an hour.

I went back to the cottages, at Primrose Row, to see the four ladies who had been witness to my accident, and got me from under the horse. I knocked at the first cottage, and said to the lady who opened the door, "Do you remember the accident here, with the runaway horse?"

She said "Yes, it was a terrible scene."

I said to her, "I'm the little girl you pulled from under the horse. I am rather late in calling on you, but I would like to thank you for saving my life."

She immediately called the other three ladies and told them "This is the little girl we saved on that terrible day, and she has called to thank us for saving her life."

They said, what a shock it was, they had not realised a child was under the horse, but they moved back a couple of yards and suddenly he raised himself again, and they saw me. Had they not moved back it may have been too late to save me before the doctor arrived; I was unconscious a long time.

There was plenty of homework to do during the week and not much time for leisure or going out. We did our homework in the middle room where there was a very large leather-topped table, with a deep drawer at both ends. It almost filled the room. Mary sat one end, and I the other, and we got on with our homework.

Mam was determined we were going to learn, and we did our best. Again there was a cupboard, glass fronted each side of the fireplace, and there were almost double the amount of books by now. The cupboards had wooden carved panels on the bottom half, glass at the top, so that we could find a book easily. The room had a three-piece suite, a gate-legged table, and bow-fronted inlaid rosewood sideboard, and a few more pieces completed the picture, not forgetting the largest mirror I ever saw above the mantelpiece. It had side arms for ornaments, and it too, was rosewood or mahogany.

After we had finished our homework, Mam put a heavy book on my head and told me I was to walk a couple of times around this large table. It would help me to "walk tall" and not slouch. I was now a very tall girl; five foot seven inches at least.

The morning, before we left for school, found Mam, with a jar of jam mixed with sulphur powder and a spoonful of that with some water to follow, was the last thing I had. This was supposed to keep "spots" (acne) at bay. I can never remember ever having a spot on my skin, not even a blemish.

Mam was very kind to us; a good understanding mother. She never thought of herself — it was always her children. Losing her own mother in childbirth, was a traumatic experience. She was only twelve years of age, at the time, and her grandmother lived with them. Together they brought up the rest of the family, until Granfer married a second time; a widow with a small baby, her husband was killed in the war. Together they had a further eight children.

A relative of my mother's was in the antique, second-hand furniture trade. He lived close by in Ynismeudw and was named Moses James. Next to his home was a huge building full of furniture. She would tell him what she was looking for, and eventually he would tell her he had the right piece for her. It was worth waiting for. Eventually this lovely house became a charming home.

Mam was always busy, and she was happy too. She hummed her favourite hymns softly to herself, but I would still be humming them too. We were alike in many ways, and singing was like a tonic to me.

My father worked the same "shift hours" as he did before "The Depression". When he worked the "night shift" 10 p.m. — 6 a.m., he would get indoors around 6.30 a.m. proceed to light the kitchen range and boil water for his bath. We did not have the bathroom at that time. For work, he wore a cotton vest, long johns, a flannel shirt — long sleeved, strong trousers and heavy toe-cap boots. A large red/white handkerchief wiped his brow from time to time and was tucked into his belt on the side of his trousers. He had very sensitive skin, and the heat of the furnaces, plus the flannel shirt inflamed his back to a mass of rash. Calamine lotion was a "must" for Dad's rash.

I was always awake when he came in. I loved listening to the dawn chorus and was soon up before he came in, and would have his water boiling for him. This meant rolling up newspapers into tight rolls, then placing sticks of wood on top (which Dad kept in the wash house), the cinders from the previous night, then fresh coal to complete the fire. Once the paper was alight, a "home-made blower" was placed in front of the fire to draw the draught and get the fire going. His clean underclothes used to hang on a rail underneath the mantelpiece from the night before, so they were "well aired". I was going along nicely, until I found a quicker way of lighting the fire. If I dipped the sticks into the paraffin can, I had a nice fire in half the time!

This went on for a while, until one morning, Mam came downstairs, saw what I had been doing, and banned me from getting up to light any more fires. She said, she could "hear" the fire roaring from upstairs and it sounded as though the chimney was alight. "If you go on like this, you will have us all burnt alive in our beds," she said. But before she banned me from lighting the fire, Dad was in from night shift and was waiting for the water to boil for his bath, which he had in front of the fire. He was smoking his pipe and half dozing. I came into the room just in time to see the legs of his long johns going up in flames. He had lit his pipe with a piece of paper, and thrown the lighted paper, not in the grate, but on his underclothes. He got the nagging that day from Mam, instead of me!!

Granfer Richards started to visit us at the Coedcae, on the occasional afternoon, (once we had left "The Graig", which was too steep for him to attempt a visit); we children looked forward to seeing him.

Granfer had remarried some years after my grandmother's death. He married a young lady who was visiting an aunt in Ynisderw Road. She was a war widow with a small son Robert. Her name was Grant. She came from Reading, Berkshire. Granfer was a good bit older than his second wife and together there were a further eight children, two girls, six boys.

His life was to change soon after the family increased. He had his first stroke. He was working on the roof of a very large building when he fell from the ladder. His foreman broke his fall, by trying to catch him, as firstly, he heard the hammer fall to the ground, and looking upwards, saw Granddad coming too.

It was a lengthy illness, before he recovered, and the second family were growing up and getting boisterous and noisy, especially the boys, who regularly sat under the table whenever he would be reading the paper, and catapulted dried peas at the back of his paper!! He could never catch them, as he was now in his late sixties.

His second stroke came seven years after his first, and he did not recover from the second one.

He would visit us to get a bit of peace from the family!! and he would always dress in a suit, hat and overcoat. Mam always went to help with the washing for the first week or so after the birth of a new baby. His second wife, was a very pleasant lady, always busy, ironing or cooking but always happy to see us.

In the parlour, first room on left of hallway through rear of the house, I remember a large wicker armchair in the corner. It was always my wish to get to it before any of the others, and this particular visit, I ran into the room, and jumped into the chair, but was soon making a terrible noise, as a nail in the side of the chair pierced my left thigh. The doctor was called for and he stitched the wound and dressed it.

Granfer's funeral was to be back to his earlier location near Gowerton, where he was born. We three granddaughters attended with Mam in deep mourning, and we stood at the graveside and listened to the preacher reading the service. The whole family were there.

Later, when relatives were leaving, I wandered off around the church, and came face to face with Granfer, I thought!? I was rooted temporarily to the spot, until the old man, spoke to me. He was Granfer's brother, who I never knew existed even, and he could have been his "twin". He was certainly "Granfer's double".

Running side on from the top of our garden, down to the main road, was the ground on which the workhouse stood. A fairly high wall divided us. Many poor people lived in there; not all of them old. Some were there, for the most trivial reasons; others homeless.

I remember one sunny afternoon, a young woman was desperately trying to climb the wall, in order to get into our garden to make her escape. My dad went up the garden to see what she was up to and after listening to her hysterical chatter, gave her a "pull up" over the wall and she made her "getaway".

Often the old men would lean on the wall and stare at us, with blank expressions. When we passed to feed the chickens or pigs, some would ask for apples. I would give them apples and plums but I never stopped to chatter, as I was scared of them.

One day, one of these old men, was standing outside the front of our house. How he got out I do not know, but after a while I found out that my young sister Enid, had told him I would take him for a walk! I hid indoors until he gave up and returned to the workhouse.

The building was used for other purposes. It had a dental clinic and maternity too. I believe it was named The Union. I attended the dental clinic there when we lived in Trebanos, as my front teeth had also been damaged in the milk float accident and were decaying at the back of the teeth. How I dreaded my visits; the injection was my fear.

One of our neighbours, Mr Thomas, was a master at the Secondary (Grammar) School and he had a son named Peter. His friend Arthur Emanuel, lived on the main road in one of a row of very nice houses laid back from the road. The two used to come up to chat to me and I sometimes played cricket! against the vicar's garage wall. They were both well mannered and polite and my parents liked them.

At the bottom of the main road, there was a small farm running down to the canal. The owners had three sons, and the local Methodist minister's sons Ceri and Dewy joined them when they came out in the evenings to chat or play games.

Near the farm was a sweet shop. They made the nicest ice cream! Their daughter Joyce, a year or two older than myself, completed our group, which met on the pavement, against the farm wall, for maybe one and a half hours at the most, after homework; just to chat, never going singly or dating. I suppose, in a way I was a little bit tomboyish! and out of this group; I was the only one going to school five miles from home. This was so, because when I passed my "11 plus", we lived on "The Graig" and the railway station was the nearest form of going to Ystalyfera. Had we been living in Raglan House, I would have gone to the Grammar in Pontardawe.

However, one evening, I joined the group beside the farm wall and on asking where Ceri was that evening, the boys remarked "Oh, he's up the road playing pocket billiards." I knew people played a game of billiards, so I accepted he was in someone's home, playing billiards.

It was later that evening when Dad said to me "Did you see all the boys this evening?" and I replied, "All except Ceri. He was up the road playing pocket billiards." I never knew why I got a clip around the head from Dad. I often wondered what the "clip" was for? "We will have none of that talk in this house" he said!

Ceri was a very good caricature artist. He was never without his slim pad and pen, and often as we chatted, he would be sketching us and I would take mine home; not that it was always complimentary, as I had a badly fractured nose! but he was so amusing. He and the older farmer's son, would have been in their late teens and the rest of us fourteen, fifteen and sixteen years old. This farmer's son never took part in our conversations but he did laugh in the right places!

Again, my sister stayed indoors. She never made local friends or friends at school and as soon as we got off the train, she would walk so fast, I was always ten or fifteen minutes later than she was, in getting home. Several times before I caught the train at Ystalyfera, one of a group of boys would run past me and snatch my cap, and would not return it, but throw it out of the window onto the railway line.

Our school uniform was extremely smart. We wore a navy-blue pleated serge tunic, with a pale-blue sash. Our long-sleeved blouse was a matching pale blue, and the tie blue and navy striped. Long black woollen stockings and black-laced shoes, together with navy gym knickers, completed the uniform. Our headgear was a navy serge cap, similar to a nurse's cap at that time. It was piped at the sides in pale blue and the school badge in the front was encircled (IYS) and also piped in blue. The blazer, navy woollen with the school badge on top left-hand pocket. It was stressed to us, we should never be seen to be improperly dressed at any time after leaving school and travelling home.

It was a very hot summer's day and as I left the train to walk the twenty minutes home, I could bear these long woollen stockings not a minute more, so I stopped and rolled them down to my ankles. Our headmaster, Mr Rees, drove through our village each school day, to Morriston, about five miles further down the valley, and the following day after Assembly, he said "Would the young lady walking home, improperly dressed in the village of Pontardawe, stay behind afterwards" and I thought I had better do so. I was told, *not* to do it again as I was letting the school down by being improperly dressed. He spoke gently and kindly to me, and asked me whether I liked my school uniform and I replied that I did, although on hot summer days, I found the woollen stockings unbearable. It was soon after that instance that our headmistress redesigned our uniform.

In winter, we wore our present uniform, *but* in summertime she gave us all the choice of wearing cotton dresses with white collars and cuffs in three colours; blue, green or beige; white ankle socks, knickers and a Panama hat. We looked extremely elegant ladies. We were allowed, she explained, to wear our gymslips "only" if we did "not feel well" or in case of accidents.

She was of stocky build, and always wore tailored costumes, thick ribbed beige stockings and brogues. She was middle aged and she taught us the French language. Her hair was worn in a tight bun. She would enter the classroom, holding a small gramophone and some books; she spoke to us in French as soon as she was settled. I loved the French language and really found no problem with the verbs and tenses; in fact, I could not wait for her to commence the lesson. But she would be infuriated when we sang *Frère Jacques*, as somebody was not singing the proper words! It was a big lad at the back of the class, who used his own version "in Welsh", for the song! The words were disgusting, but as she did not know any Welsh — she did not know what this version meant! The melody being the same, everyone in the class had a job to keep a straight face, as he sang these dreadful words out loud, with gusto. He was, in turn, regularly tormented by our strict Science Master, Mr Bell, who was rather a nice person, very conscientious, and no problem to students who paid attention to his lesson. He was also much taller than the lad, and would explode "People see this boy coming to school daily, weighed down by the heavy satchel on his back. Full of books they think; let me enlighten them, half the books are still at home, were they but to know, it is full of sandwiches. No wonder you can't follow the lesson! You are half asleep!"

My sister, Mary, was extremely good at Needlework and Crochet. She would crochet fine lace tablecloths or chairbacks. I can remember Mam saying she could use her treasured "Singer" sewing machine, which was Mam's pride and joy. Mary made herself some blouses and dresses and she made me a dress too. When our Confirmation Day arrived, both our dresses were made in cream silk. She would have been about fourteen years of age, no more, and she made them very well. My dress was plain, long sleeved, with the usual "Peter Pan" collar. Mary's was a "Two-Piece" with a peplum waist.

I had just started my periods, and knew very little about this stage in my life. I only knew what "Joyce" had told me. "Oh! it's terrible. Now you've started, it will get worse and worse until it pours from you!" Imagine my horror, this was supposed to go on until I was fifty! How was I going to cope? I didn't think I could. It so happened to arrive on the day of my Confirmation, and I did not feel too well and told Joyce. We both sat in church, waiting for the service to start. She was sitting next to me and I was very nervous. When the bishop arrived, and the service started, we were to walk up to the altar, a row at a time, to be confirmed. Imagine my distress as I rose from my seat, Joyce whispered, "Oh! it's all on the back of your dress." I was horrified and wished the floor would open and swallow me up. Instead, I put both my hands at the back of my dress and slowly walked to the altar. I returned in the same way, hiding the back of my dress with my hands.

When the service was over, I was the first out of the church, and I ran, like I never knew I could, all the way home, a good fifteen minutes. I ripped off the dress and cried. There wasn't a spot on it, and I had been in such a state all the afternoon. How could Joyce have done that to me? This was my failing, I believed whatever people told me. My father always introduced me as "The one who has to learn the hard way," and my sister Mary as "The Lady of the House!!" Now I could see why.

It was 1935, and celebrations were in preparation for the Silver Jubilee of King George V and Queen Mary. There was a huge beacon on top of the Barley and Mary and I asked whether we could go. Mam agreed, but we had to be home by ten o'clock.

We went with Peter and Arthur. I was with Arthur, a tall slim boy, very polite and I liked him a lot. Mary walked with Peter, he was shorter, a little tubby and very jolly. We had a great time, we met lots of other teenagers we knew, but we forgot all about the time. However, it was turning cold now and we asked the "time" of a man walking by. "Midnight" he said. My God, were we scared? We were afraid almost to go home.

We made our way down the rocky hillside; the path was very narrow. I was sheltering under Arthur's jacket (although he was wearing it) when I saw my father's outline coming up the side of the hill towards us. "Where the hell have you been?" he said and "What time do you call this?" Before we could open our mouths he said "Get on home and to bed, before your mother sees you" and turning to the two boys he said, "And you can clear off, before I kick your . . . ." I felt so ashamed, how could he be so common? He never spoke to us in that manner. He never swore and neither did we.

When we got home, once indoors, he said, "Get up to bed quickly before your mother wakes up, or you'll be for it." That was the only time I can remember my dad speaking sharply to us. He was always so jolly.

The two lads became doctors when they grew up and were at the same hospital in Cardiff. All I remember of that night was the humiliation I felt.

The hill on the opposite side of the valley was called "Alltwen". We could see from our house, and hear, a Scotsman "playing the bagpipes". He came every year at a certain time; playing for several hours. The music would echo across the valley. Then later on, he would come down from the hillside and knock on the doors, and ask whether you could spare a coin? His music was joy, and in fact, I wished he did not go away.

Like Mam, I was frightened of snakes, and one day, a very hot sunny afternoon, I went along the path at the side of the house, to get some milk from a farm five minutes' walk away. I was suddenly petrified; there, on the bank of the hill, on a large stone, were several snakes, entwined in the sun. They lay there — one mass of sparkling colour, and they were large snakes. I did not go for the milk that day. I don't even know how I got back home!

By now, Mary and I had changed our mode of travelling to school, and were travelling by bus, which we joined at the foot of our road. It saved the twenty minutes' walk each way to the station daily.

Living at the other side of the workhouse at Ynismeudw was a school chum, named Iris Evans, and one morning, she joined me at the bus stop, satchel slung over her shoulder, and both hands holding a large box. I looked at her, and smilingly said, "It's got to be a cake or sandwiches, Iris?"

She said, "Oh no; it's a whopping big snake!"

"I don't wish to see it," I said, feeling goose pimples creeping over me.

So she said, "Well, I'll tell you how I got it."

Her mother and father were both gardening the previous evening, the garden being on a higher level to the house, and assessable by a dozen steps, when her mother screamed "Oh God, there is the biggest snake I have ever seen!" Her father ran to help her mother, who was practically hysterical. He slashed at the snake with his scythe, and so they continued to work on, until they had finished gardening for the evening.

They were indoors later that evening eating dinner (all seated around the kitchen table) when her mother, again said "What is that under the table?" She had felt something on her foot.

Looking down, they saw this same snake, dragging himself along the floor! He never got a second chance. Her father killed it.

And here was Iris, by now with the lid half off and me about to faint! He was as large as the one which was thrown over a branch earlier at our home. She was taking this snake to the school laboratory, possibly to be preserved.

F

My sister, I remember, put a small snake in a large preserving bottle with earth, and she told me that snakes eat the earth, then eliminated it, this being the reason for the small *round-shaped* earth bits the next day? There were many small snakes from time to time down below in the "currant garden". I would wear wellingtons when I had to pick the currants.

Mam loved the garden. Dad would grow large cabbages and in-between each in the rows, would be Mam's flowers. She had her flowerbeds, but she could never resist stealing some of Dad's plot! Her salad beds were very much admired, and she often cut some of the lettuce, spring onions, etc., and left them outside the front of the house, for whoever had wished for fresh greens. She was so kind, "We have more than enough" she would explain.

Eighty per cent of our neighbours living on the Coedcae were professional men.

Chapter Five

I would have been, possibly thirteen years of age, and Mam would be forty-three, when she developed eczema on both her arms, from her elbows to her fingers, and at the back of her knees. She suffered agony from constant irritation. The scabbed surface was very dry but broken, and she tried an ointment called Zambuk. It soothed the irritation and took some of the heat out of the sores. The disease seemed to come suddenly, coupled with fainting attacks. Of course, we did not know the reason for the change in her health. The light in her eyes dimmed, she was in a lot of pain, and all the sleeves, she cut from her dresses, the weight of a sleeve even (mainly cotton) was too much. It restricted her from going outdoors. She was adamant, "No doctor" — yet she called the doctor if we so much as ran a temperature at all.

Both Mary and I were immediately shown how to make bread, cakes and daily meals. We also took over the washing and cleaning, changing over the chores each week. Everything was home cooked as before, and if Dad was on night shift 10 p.m. — 6 a.m., many times I got up in the night to find Mam sitting by a dying fire, quietly crying. I would say "Don't cry Mam."

"But I can't cry in the daytime" she would say. "It would upset you all."

After several years it cleared, but Mam went through a lot of pain.

Then Dad made us a "dolly" for the heavy washing. After all the washing for the week was done — with a large tub standing on two chairs — we took it in turns to use the rubbing board and lifted the tub to the floor when we would then shake the coal dust from Dad's working clothes (flannel shirts etc.,) outside in the yard and soak them in the tub for a while before swishing them to and fro with the "dolly". It was a long-handled wooden piece with a square bottom. It had four wooden legs. Then later, the same performance in the rinsing water, before hanging out to dry. We did the extra work willingly. We wanted our Mam to get back to her cheerful self — if only she had seen the doctor earlier.

Saturday nights, I was allowed to meet up with friends in the village. Una, was my best friend. Her parents had a "high-class" shoe shop in the High Street, and Una was usually free after 6.30 p.m. — not that she worked in the shop. She had hobbies. Her favourite pastime was the piano, and I would join her, sitting in the parlour, waiting whilst she practised a piece. Her mother, was my mam's friend from when they were young ladies, and before they married. The moment I appeared on the doorstep, she would call out from the shop, "Kathleen, go in dear, Una's doing this or that." It was always a pleasant greeting, and after Una had a final "look in the mirror", we were off!

We would make straight to the lower end of Herbert Street, to Sabers fish and chip shop first, where Una would remove her fresh piece of chewing gum, and enjoy a large portion of chips, then in with the chewing gum and we were off. The "two smart girls" they called us. We would stop and chat to some lads, again mostly lads from outside farms who wore their best clothes and visited the big-time Pontardawe on "Saturday Nights". We never went for walks, just laughed and chatted, got up to date with any news, and of course at night-time, the village looked more attractive than daytime, and so we would say goodbye and perhaps meet some more lads and again chat for a while, but not if my father was outside the crossroads. He would ask me "Where are you going?"

I'd say "Just walking around."

"Not with that lipstick on your lips," he'd say. "Wipe it off this minute."

He would hand me his clean handkerchief and I would clean my lips, but as soon as we said goodbye, I would stand in a doorway and put it back on again!

Mam had warned me to be in early one Saturday night, as a girl had recently been murdered in some part of Swansea, and that was only eight miles away from us. I was just about to leave the house when I heard spine chilling screams coming from the "Barley" at the rear of the house. I ran back indoors and got Mam and my young sister to stand outside and listen. Again we heard screams and it most certainly sounded as though a woman was being murdered that night.

Mam turned to me and said "You are passing the police station on your way to the village — call in and report it."

The station had a section house, so that meant plenty of men to carry out a search. This I did, and they all listened intently. Then several policemen went to the hillside with lanterns and torches to look for the victim. They were on the Barley hillside for hours but they found nothing.

It was some days later, when I was up early as Dad came in from his night shift. He called me outside the house towards the garden, and we heard the screams again. Looking up at the skyline, on the rock above the hillside, was a vixen and she was making those terrible screams.

Dad looked at me and said "Was that what you heard the other night?" I said "Yes, exactly."

"Then you heard a vixen calling for her mate," he said.

We solved the riddle of the missing "body" ourselves.

While we lived at Raglan House, my dad was taken ill with quinsy. He was very ill at the time and stayed in bed for a couple of weeks. I remember there was a strange atmosphere as we crept around, keeping as quiet as we could, not to disturb him. He started to recover, once the quinsy had burst. He wasn't often ill. He was a strong man; about five foot seven inches tall. Thickset was the description which would fit him. He wasn't fat at all; he was of very smart appearance. He had a good head of thick wavy hair, forming a widow's peak (Libra sign) on his forehead. When he dressed to go out, he picked a small tea rose to put in his lapel; they were plentiful in the garden. He was popular in the village. He liked a game of billiards and played in The Public Hall. He could speak the Welsh language perfectly, better than we could! He was an Irishman, and learnt the language at night school and he would correct us if we used a "slang" word for something, instead of the proper one.

For as long as I can remember, when Dad combed his hair, he would complain of a small lump on the top of his head. The comb would sometimes catch on this lump and hurt him.

He must have been complaining about it one day and none of us showed interest in "this lump" so he disappeared upstairs with the mirror from the side of the back door. Imagine the horror, when he reappeared in the living room doorway later that afternoon, with blood pouring down his face. We all thought he had tried to commit suicide, but all he would say was "I've done it. I've done it. It's out!" He had taken two mirrors and his "open razor" upstairs, and he had cut out this lump from the "top of his head!".

Mam sent me two doors away, to use the telephone. I was to ask the doctor to come straight away, before he "bled to death!".

In the meantime, Mam stuck a bath towel on the top of his head, and told him to keep it there!

The doctor duly arrived and examined the wound, then gave a loud "belly laugh". He placed a yellow coloured gauze dressing on it and remarked "I couldn't have done a better job myself."

My mam often had premonitions. We girls laughed at her, until, uncannily we realised she was not teasing us. Then it so happened a friend of the family, living on the opposite hill of Alltwen, passed away, and as is the custom in Wales, they have a "funeral tea", where all the female relatives and friends, sit down, and partake of sandwiches, cold meats and cake, whilst the cortege goes to the church and cemetery. Women don't normally go to the funeral. When the men return, the table has been relaid with food for them and the women retreat into the parlour to continue conversing together.

Alltwen was separated from us by the River Tawe and the canal.

Mam got in touch with her brother and his wife and offered to do the sandwiches, etc., but was told one of the ladies in the road had taken on the duty.

The night before the funeral, Mam dreamt she was looking down from a height at "dirty water". "A bad omen" she said. We passed it off lightly but sure enough she was contacted that morning and asked whether she would still be available to see to the "funeral tea", as the lady who had so kindly offered to do it, had thrown herself into the canal near the "Bridge" in Herbert Street, Pontardawe, and drowned. The water was murky and green.

A second experience, was my time spent in hospital at Oystermouth, at the "Working Men's Home", taken over by the Swansea Hospital as their annexe. A lady opposite me, was desperately ill with cancer. She was allowed visitors freely. Soon after I left, my mother again had a dream. I was accompanying her to Ammanford, roughly eight miles away by bus, with a sheaf of flowers to a new estate. It was a funeral, and the mourners and friends were packed into the hallway and onto the lawn outside. She said the coffin was at the end of the hall and she could see there were three handles, not two as was custom on those days, each side of the coffin. I had suspicions of duodenal ulcer at the time and this found me sharing the same ward with the lady who was so ill. And so we were not surprised when a letter from her husband arrived telling me his wife had passed away, the day of the funeral, and their address in Ammanford.

Mam and I travelled to her address and experienced every detail of Mam's dream. There were so many friends and relatives they had to stand outside on the front lawn, and she lay in her coffin in the hall.

We always had a pet, a dog and a cat, but our latest dog was killed by trotting down from Raglan House, and springing up onto the lawn of a house facing the main road. I had gone on an errand earlier to Joyce Thomas's shop and when I came out of the shop, he must have seen me and came across amid the busy traffic. The owner of the house helped me to carry him back home, where he was buried in the garden.

So when Mam was asked by our next door neighbour, who was a vicar, Reverend Ezical Hopkins, if she would look after his dog, while he went to a conference in Bristol with his wife, Mam agreed; the dog knew us anyway — and settled in immediately. He was a white bull terrier, but there was a strange thing about this dog. It was summertime and the dog lay around the house most of the day, but about 7 p.m. each evening, it disappeared, although it came back again around 8 p.m. We thought nothing of it, but this routine went on for the best part of the week.

However, one evening, a couple of policemen called at our house and enquired whether the dog was ours? Mam explained, the owners were away and we were looking after it.

"Well, we are afraid Madam, this dog has been caught *worrying sheep*," they said, and they asked Dad to accompany them to the vicar's rear garden, where they immediately dug a large hole in the ground and threw in a lump of raw meat. As the dog jumped into the hole, they shot it, then covered him up. They then contacted the vicar to let him know what they had done. They told us, that the dog had been seen to wash the blood off himself, by rolling in a stream, before returning to our house!

Chapter Six

The year of 1938 saw me out of Grammar School (IYS) at Ystalyfera, and trying to make up my mind what I was going to do. Temporarily that is! I had done quite well, (so Mam and Dad said) especially in Language, Maths, Art and Science.

I was restless, until one day, I saw an application in the window of the local "Home and Colonial" food stores for a cashier. Arithmetic to me was like music, so I immediately walked in, only to learn from the manager, "The position has just been filled. I'm so sorry," he said.

I continued down Herbert Street, and again I saw "Cashier Wanted". The shop was "John Bull Stores". I walked in and was given the position immediately. It was a "fill in" position for another member of the staff — who was sick. My wages were eight shillings (40p) per week, and on Fridays and Saturdays, I was expected to check the large orders of groceries the public bought in the evenings (both evenings) before paying at the cash desk. Most of the week would be fairly quiet.

Beside the manager, there was one young girl, Miss Myfanwy Daniels, who mainly weighed various foods such as dried fruit (currants, raisins, sultanas, glacé cherries, etc.), sugar, flour and so on. She spent most of her time in the warehouse at the rear of the shop, sitting next to the sack of whatever she was packing into ½lbs or 1lbs in weight, *besides* sampling all she weighed! Another assistant served at the counter. He was quite reliable and well mannered.

A young lad in his early teens delivered the groceries by trolley, should they be too heavy for the customer to carry, i.e. Fridays and Saturdays.

How was I going to tell Mam, I had a job. She was against it from the start. "Grammar School, and you end up in a food shop like John Bull Stores!" She refused to accept any of my wages. I stressed over and over again, it's only temporary, as I would never have found it a satisfactory position, after having a good education. But it was a laughable experience with regard to some situations which occurred there!

Friday nights (open until 8 p.m.) saw me standing behind the assistant, who had a vast order of groceries ready for checking pricewise. His pencil was already sharpened for listing the goods to arrive at the total, whereas, I moved each commodity to the right, adding up mentally and audibly, as I went along, when I would arrive at the total, jot it down, then to "Double Check", I would pass each commodity to the left side and add up to reach the total. If it was the same, the customer was happy to start packing her groceries into her bags and I was much quicker than the old "pencil".

Miss Daniels, could not resist the chocolate mallows, or the coconut mallows, and her pockets would hold as many as they would take. No one bothered about it. The manager, "Danny" said, "She will soon get sick of them."

One day I walked into the warehouse and she was sitting on a stool, a scoop in her hand and on her face, a look of desperation! I said "Anything wrong?"

She said "Yes, I feel sick and also I need the toilet," which was above the shop, but the only way to reach it was to leave the store, pass the butchers next door to us, and at the rear of the butchers were steps leading up to the empty flat to the lavatories.

I said, "I think you should go straight away, it can only become worse if you don't."

She did get there in time, although it did not deter her from eating while she weighed the goods. I reckon, she ate as much as she got in wages each week!

The young lad who delivered the groceries Friday nights, lived nearby in Thomas Street. A likeable boy, polite, energetic and always on time.

Saturday mornings, saw Miss Daniels in her best attire, for the evening to follow. I don't know where she went. She was an attractive girl, and with three cinemas in the village, there was a choice of films. Her brother John and elder sister went to the same High School as I did.

However, this particular Saturday morning, we were walking along Grove Road and had almost reached Thomas Street, when we met up with the delivery lad, pushing the empty trolley back to the shop after Friday evening's delivery. We had reached the bridge when Miss Daniels exploded "Please let me have a ride on the trolley down the steep bridge?" In no time she had spread herself across the trolley, legs stretched out in front. I thought to myself, 'I hope she does not get any oil on her new coat' which was a light strawberry colour.

When she reached the bottom of the hill, below the bridge, she found one side of her coat was trapped in the wheel of the trolley! We managed to wriggle her out of her coat, but the coat was torn and very oily! "Oh God, my mam will kill me" she squealed. "What can I do?"

I suggested we call at the dry cleaners and get the opinion of the manageress, who said "Leave it with me. I'll try and clean it." She did an excellent job, by hand, having to sew the torn part first, then sponging off the oil. So her mother did not kill her that time!

We had one hour for lunch — 1 p.m.-2 p.m. the shop closed. It was a twenty minute walk home for me. The last part uphill and the same time back. If the lunch was ready I had time to eat something, but one day, a scruffy, noisy van, with a backfiring exhaust, had just delivered the meat to the butchers, next door. I asked the driver which direction he was going in. He said "Ystalyfera," so he would be passing the bottom of the road I lived at.

"Could you give me a lift please," I asked "and drop me off near the workhouse?" That would give me extra time to have a meal.

"Fine, hop in," he said, but he insisted it was no trouble to drive me to the top of our road, drop me off and be away again.

I shall never forget the look on Mam's face and some of our neighbours, mainly professional people, when I got out of the van. She said "That is enough! Either you pack in that job or you take sandwiches." So sandwiches it was, for a few more weeks.

The weekly eight shillings I earned, was put in a jug inside the grandmother clock on the wall, and it grew each week, as Mam kept her word and would not touch it.

Morning and afternoon tea breaks were about 15—20 minutes, so I would "pop out" and have a chat with some of the butcher's family or preferably I enjoyed tormenting "Jim Rengozzi", who was in charge of the tearoom-cum-ice-cream parlour, they owned in Herbert Street. A very respected family. Jim's face was often to be seen looking through the "hatchway" at the entrance to the restaurant, but I had a strong crush on Jim. I believe he was mid-forties, older than my dad. It was not sex ways, but I could not resist that smile, and I would torment him! He hardly ever said a word to me. He probably thought I needed a spanking. I was, cheeky is the word! He had two brothers, younger than himself, and they were both in the Fire Brigade. His parents had passed on, so he was the head of the family apart from one sister, Mary, who was single. She wore thick glasses and never smiled; not at me anyway!

However, one day, he did ask me whether I would like a "cup of tea".

I said "Yes please, if there's time."

The hot water came from the expresso boiler, plus a tea bag and a drop of milk.

I was about to drink my tea, when his sister, Mary, came through the "swing door", looked at me most aggressively, and spoke to Jim in Italian. So I got up and left. I'm sure he got a "dressing down" when I had gone!

I would still rest my chin on my side of the hatchway, whenever I saw his face there, and if it was my break, I would perhaps ask him whether he had "pots of money", and if he had, where would he take me? And he would have a fit of the giggles. He would have a job to stop giggling. I asked him again and told him, "Actually I've always fancied Paris!!" That made him giggle even more. I don't believe Jim spoke more than a dozen words to me in all the times I joined him at the hatchway! Then I would promise to be good and leave him alone. Basically, he was very shy, although he would look into my face and me his; I would smile, he would giggle!

I left the shop where I worked soon after. I was about sixteen years old now.

When the headlines in the newspapers carried the story of "King Edward and Mrs Simpson", Una asked me whether I would like to go to my first dance.

It was a private party. I wore a very nice dress and I had my hair quite short, shaped into the back of my neck and parted down the middle and close to my ears. More than once, whilst dancing, I heard remarks "Oh doesn't that young lady look like Mrs Simpson," until I felt a little peeved, and I said to Una, "I don't look like Mrs Simpson surely, do I?"

A gentleman, partnering his lady friend, in a loud voice said, "Yes you do love, but don't look so sad — she's just nabbed the King of England!"

It was about this time, a family moved into our road. They had two daughters, Mary and Rhoda, and an aged aunt. Together the five lived lower down our road. Their surname was Baggott. The father owned two of the three cinemas in our village — "The Lyric" and "The Public Hall". There was a third, "The Pavilion", but that was owned by someone else.

The younger daughter, Mary, was in the ticket booth at "The Lyric", and auntie was an usherette in "The Public Hall". They asked me whether I could help them out in the evenings, for just a couple of weeks, as they had two major pictures coming along, which would be shown for a whole week each. I agreed. Little did I know what "auntie" had in store for me!

The picture showing for the first week was "The Mikado" and by the time she had finished with me, I was "dressed up" as a "Geisha" girl and I wore a large chrysanthemum in my hair. She even expected me to "shuffle" along with short steps when I showed patrons to their seats!

By the end of the week, my head was ringing with the music of The Mikado, and it kept me awake at nights; even though my body was tired, my mind was not.

The following week, for the whole week, the picture was "Gunga Din". By the time the week was up, it had put me off the cinema for ages, and looking back, I received no wages. My work was taken as "complimentary".

It was wintertime and "The Public Hall" was freezing cold. I stood with my back to the radiator, once the film was well settled, but was soon told by Auntie to keep away from the heaters; "It isn't that cold!"

At both cinemas, but different nights, a young man, named Jacky Evans, worked for the Baggott family. He worked quite hard and was always being told to do this, then do that, and quickly. I felt sorry for him. He was so pleased to be helpful. He had a nervous laugh, coupled with a big smile, and often a giggle, but he was kind and good.

The first night after the show ended, I stepped outside the cinema, and the darkness was frightening. I thought of the twenty-minute walk home, either over the canal bridge and up Grove Road, or up to the village crossroads, and along the main road. The branch road to the Coedcae was creepy at any night, especially at the top where we lived. So the next evening I asked Jacky whether he knew where the Coedcae was, and he did, so I asked him whether he would accompany me home to my gate, each evening whilst I worked for the Baggotts?

"Yes Miss Healy, of course Miss Healy," he said, and this he did, much to the annoyance of "Auntie" who expected him to work a further hour whilst she "cashed up" for the night, or would I make it easier all round by staying the extra hour and have her company home. I refused vehemently.

They were folk you could never get to know, or get close to. It was business only and their way only.

It was now 1939, and Mam insisted we both take a crash course in shorthand/typewriting and book-keeping, nearby in a private house, in Grove Road, Pontardawe, as war seemed imminent. It was named "Glanffrwd". Our master was Mr George. It was a two-year course, which you paid for in advance, although we both completed and passed the examinations in eight months.

Mam did not want us to be directed into "Work of Importance", as it may have been a manual job in munitions, so seeing adverts for secretaries in Government offices, we did as she thought best and Mary took up a position as a shorthand typist at the Air Ministry in Wiltshire. She worked with other young secretaries in a beautiful ladies' college known as Westonbirt, and billeted with three others outside in the local village.

She was not happy there, so she moved to Stroud, in Gloucestershire, and to the Meteorological Office at Stonehouse, where she stayed for the period she spent with the Air Ministry; three years.

It was at this time, April 1940, that I, too, joined the Air Ministry in Stroud, Gloucestershire. I was almost seventeen years of age and ready to start my work which was to bring me up to the age of twenty-one years.

Before taking on the appointment, Mam took me to Swansea and kitted me out with extra clothing, especially "three of everything" in underclothes, using the family clothing coupons to do so; plus a nice thick coat to keep me warm. Once my new case was packed, I was ready to leave for Stroud.

Sadly, Mam looked at me, and said, "You be a good girl and work hard to make something of yourself, and *don't* you dare bring any trouble home here."

I hadn't a clue what trouble meant. I thought it was, sitting on a toilet seat, without *covering* the seat with paper, and possibly catching "the bad disease!"

With these words ringing in my ears, I kissed her goodbye, caught the bus to Swansea at the bottom of our road, and then on by train to Stroud, in Gloucestershire; where for the next four years, I was to work and grow up.

'My Childhood Home'

I remember the stone house at the top of the hill,
I was eleven when we moved in; it stands there still.
The walls were thick, eighteen inches my mother used to boast,
She would know, Granfer was a stonemason and better than most!
His handiwork, stands as a monument so grand —
Elementary and Grammar Schools, houses too, made by hands;
Not smooth and soft but weathered and hard,
Proud of his trade — he worked very hard.
This house was big, with plenty of ground,
For keeping chickens and pigs around.
I remember too, the rooms inside —
The kitchen, the middle room and parlour besides.
The pantry, a room so big, the shelves on the wall,
Held most kinds of preserves.
The slab where the pigs, once slaughtered were salted,
Had been there for years, for the salt it had now spread,
To the wall which adjoined it, and showed through the paper;
To cure such a problem, the wall came down later.
We hopped and we jumped through the "hole in the wall",
Enjoying the fun, but a nuisance to all,
The slab was discarded, a new wall rebuilt;
The parlour repapered, and we kept "no more pigs".
I liked the old house, it was nice, it was sunny,
But at night, I was frightened, and it wasn't so funny.
I slept on my own in a big airy bed,
I often was scared and covered my head.
I'd looked in the cupboards, and saw nothing there,
But nevertheless, I was still very scared.
Three decades have passed, since I last saw the house,
But drawn by an urge, I was very aroused,
To relive my youth, and to take "just a peep",
I never expected, a lady to meet,
Who noticed the interest which showed in my face,
"Come in," she said kindly. "Look over the place."
The rooms now looked bigger and brighter by far,
The 'old ranges' had gone, to make the rooms large.
Though much had been done to improve every room,
The familiar child's image, disappeared quite soon.
I was happy to wander all over the place,
But — the house I remembered, now had a new face.
"Raglan House" it was called, it had a good image,
And stood so imposing at the top of the village.
But as years rolled away, its name is no more,
It now has a number, it's now thirty-four!

'Mother'

Often when I sit and ponder, of my childhood long ago,
Mother's face, stands clear before me; life for her was quite a chore.
Father, kind and gentle to us, tried so hard to look for work,
But the times were hard and hungry, for 'most others too were hurt.
"The Depression" was a period, when a lot of people found,
That the stress which rained upon them, made the men look all around.
Trying hard to earn a "penny", Father helped around the farms,
But not everyone was lucky, we had food, we were not harmed.
Mother's hair grew white from worry, never knowing day to day,
What the "morrow" would be bringing, till a man called in to say,
Five years unemployment ended — from the steelworks nearby,
Work at last there was for Father, proudly he brought home his "pay".
Life had dealt her many sorrows, which she overcame alone,
Keeping strains and stresses from us, making us a happy home.
She had nursed me in my childhood, taught me all the rights from wrongs,
Helped me grow up like a lady,
How I miss her, now she's gone.

'The Boy I knew at School'

This boy at school was such a fool, though he thought he was clever;
He always sat at the back of the class
And do his homework — Never!
He had excuses all the time, his satchel — proud as punch,
Would weigh him down, but we were told
'Twas full of daily lunch!
He never seemed to make the grade, but was quite good at Welsh,
The words he sang for "Frère Jacques"
Were never sung in French!
I asked around after the war, I'd heard no more of him,
A very brave courageous man,
His praises they would sing.
He had no fear but did his job, dropping from the sky,
Whilst all around him guns did fire,
You could not him decry.
He may have failed his studies young, but courage he had plenty,
And medals too, there were quite a few;
This boy he was but twenty!
You can't judge him by what he knew, you'd not say he was learned,
Put to the test — he was the best,
'Twas men like him who saved us.

The author — at seventy-six